The Art of Contentment

The Art of Contentment

ROBERT H. KLIMA

foreword by Tim MacGowan

RESOURCE *Publications* · Eugene, Oregon

THE ART OF CONTENTMENT

Resource Publications
An Imprint of Wipf and Stock Publishers
199 W. 8th Ave., Suite 3
Eugene, OR 97401

www.wipfandstock.com

PAPERBACK ISBN: 979-8-3852-0446-5
HARDCOVER ISBN: 979-8-3852-0447-2
EBOOK ISBN: 979-8-3852-0448-9

VERSION NUMBER 12/04/23

Dedicated to the memory of my mother

Pauline Mason Klima

1919-2010

Who always loved and never complained

Contents

Foreword

Reading the insights of "the saints who've gone before" from various centuries and contexts reminds me that the basics of the Christian faith don't change from generation to generation. Take the search for contentment or happiness, where our world is filled with roadmaps that claim to help us to find the way. And this search is not just a contemporary one. We may imagine that contentment was easier to find in an earlier historical moment, before the complications of our time, but Scripture reveals that this is not so. The Apostle Paul writes of learning the secret of contentment (Philippians 4:6). Discovering that secret is worth the effort because "godliness with contentment is great gain" (1 Timothy 6:6).

Yet for Christians today, the definition – let alone the realization – of contentment is so radically different from what our culture presents, that we benefit from ancient guidance as we try to find our way. The unnamed author of *The Art of Contentment*, writing centuries ago, reminds us of this reality: true contentment is both possible and desirable. I found the author's succinct insights completely applicable to my modern life. For example, he writes in the preface:

Another man thinks that happiness is found in minerals, so he digs for it until he is covered with clay and finds a grave where he sought his treasure.

What a vivid picture – the pursuit of happiness in the wrong direction leads me to dig my own grave!

I found great profit in slowly reading and meditating on the timeless truths that this short book offers. In 12 concise chapters (just 153 numbered paragraphs), the author encourages and exhorts fellow believers to identify and pursue a biblical contentment that will nourish anxious souls. I read a paragraph or two each day as part of my devotional routine, and would urge any believer to do the same.

My friend Bob Klima has done a great service for those of us who will read this work by carefully and faithfully updating the language, while allowing the wisdom of earlier centuries to find its voice in ours. Thank you Bob.

I pray that the gift of contentment would grow in you as you digest this banquet.

Tim MacGowan

Introduction

THE BOOK ENTITLED *The Whole Duty of Man* is an English Protestant devotional work which was first published in 1658. It was very popular in its day. That was a difficult time in England. The English Civil War ran from 1642 until 1651, and was primarily a contest between Parliament and King Charles I over who had and should have power and authority in the Kingdom. Parliament prevailed and Charles was executed. Thereafter, Parliament established a Commonwealth and Oliver Cromwell, a military and government leader during the war, became the primary leader of the new government. In 1660, the monarchy was reestablished under King Charles II, two years after Cromwell's death.

But the English Civil War was also about religion. Various Protestant groups, primarily the Anglicans, the Puritans and Presbyterians, fought over which should become the official church of England. Each sought to be recognized by the government as the only legal church and to have the government sanction its prayer book as the only acceptable prayer book in the land. And in this religious conflict, many people were killed. It is not surprising that the author of *The Whole Duty of Man* should choose to remain anonymous. It is entirely possible that he may have been persecuted or even killed for his views. So no name is given for the author in the original edition. No less than 27 possible authors of the work have been suggested, among them Richard Allestree and Humphrey Henchman.

Several other works later appeared as having been written by "the author of *The Whole Duty of Man*," including a book entitled *The Art of Contentment*, which was first published in 1675. I obtained an original edition of the book printed in the year 1700. I was impressed by the value of the work and believe it to be as relevant today as it was when it was written. The book is, however, written in a very quaint old English style, which makes it difficult to read for many people.

I thought that it might be useful to rewrite the work into modern English, so that the valuable material in it might be more easily read and appreciated. The following is my attempt to do so. The original consists of twelve sections. Each section is in numbered paragraphs. I have tried to faithfully rewrite each numbered paragraph in the original order. I have not added any personal commentary to it, but have tried to remain as faithful as possible to what I believe to be the original content of the work. In doing so, I have had to make decisions when to stay close the the original wording and when a larger rewriting, or paraphrase, would better reflect the original intent. At the same time, I have tried to maintain the feel of the book as much as possible. I only hope that my attempt will be sufficient to convey the material effectively.

ROBERT H. KLIMA

SECTION I

Of the Necessary Connection between Happiness and Contentment

1. God is essentially happy in and of Himself. He cannot be made more happy because of anything men may do. He did not make men for the purpose of increasing His happiness. Instead, He made men that He might communicate His happiness to them. This is His original plan and it is shown in all of His actions towards them. When man by his sin defeated this purpose, causing endless misery, God restored His original purpose, through His mercy, by the death of His Son. And in addition to this, He has given other methods to rational people. He has shown us what we must avoid and He has shown us a picture of Heaven as our goal. He has shown us a level and pleasant path which leads to Heaven.

2. By doing this, God has not only secured our ultimate happiness, but our happiness here on earth as well. Those Christian duties which He has given us are not only to carry us to Heaven but are intended also to refresh us here. The Christian faith is the art of happy living. Its very tasks are rewards. Its commands are to increase our true pleasures.

3.   Happiness is an actual expression of every Christian duty and is found in the willful acceptance of the duty. Happiness and contentment are essentially the same thing. To ask us to be content is the same thing as to ask us to be happy.

4.   All of the earthly things which we enjoy, such as pleasure, wealth and honor, which we think make us happy are rightly rejected by thinking persons for this reason: They come from outside us and may be taken away or withheld from us. The very possession of them is precarious. For this reason, seeking after them makes us unhappy. Happiness must exist in the mind and in the soul and cannot be based upon our fortune. Happiness is found in the practice of virtue, which in itself is good and makes those who possess it good.

5.   The Greek philosopher Epictetus summarized our moral duty in two words, to sustain and to abstain; that is, to bear with constancy adverse events, and with moderation to enjoy prosperity. This idea is expressed in the single concept of contentment, which involves patiently bearing misfortune and having great contempt for inappropriate sensual choices. The Greeks called this state of mind "self-sufficiency." We know this to be an essential attribute of God, which He cannot pass on to us. But the Christian faith instead declares, as Paul said, that he learned how to want and how to abound, and in whatever state he happens to be in, therewith to be content: He is able to do all things through Christ who strengthens him, Philippians 4:11, 12-13, and "having nothing, to possess all things." 2 Corinthians 6:10.

6.   This great condition comes about because all good things come from God, and anyone who by virtue and faith comes to possess them, thereby has everything. From a human point of view, the Greek philosopher Plato rightly observed that happiness does not come from increasing possessions, but from lessening desires. And from that observation, it follows that a contented person considers himself to be abundantly provided for, is entirely satisfied with what he

has, and desires nothing more. And it has been correctly said of those who covet, that they want what they do not possess more than they want what they do possess. But a contented person is just the opposite of this: he enjoys what he has and is happy because he is not always wanting something else.

7. If one does not have the grace of contentment, he does not have the power by his success or his affluence to make life seem tolerable. If anyone had everything which he desired, he would be pressed to death by the sheer weight of it. He who has what is necessary to be happy but cannot be satisfied with it is more miserable than he who does not have them; for he who has nothing hopes to have something, but he who has enough but does not enjoy what he has, can only think of wanting more.

8. Therefore, anyone who seeks the essence of happiness must find it in contentment. When contentment is separated from possessions, it is not diminished when those possessions pass away. The Apostle Paul said that he was content in any situation, and his contentment did not depend on his circumstances. Anyone who understands the difference between the earthly and the eternal will agree with the prophet, "although the fig tree shall not blossom, neither shall fruit be in the vines, the labor of the olive shall fail, and the fields yield not meat; the flocks shall be cut from the fold, and there shall be no herds in the stall; yet will I rejoice in the Lord. I will joy in the God of my salvation." Habakkuk 3:17-18. Whoever has God should not be disappointed by the lack of anything else. Anyone who considers the bounty and glory of our future home, should not be discouraged by the lack of anything in this home.

9. Because God is sensitive to our weaknesses, and knows how impatient we are by nature, and how unlikely we are to walk "by faith and not by sight," 2 Corinthians 5:7, He gives us a taste of satisfaction here. He gives us earthly blessings

universally although not equally. Even the least of us has cause to be thankful. While no one has all he wants, yet he has more than what he complains that he wants; and he has much that he would not willingly give up.

10.   From this, we should expect mankind to be cheerful; when we consider what a blessed end we shall have and what blessings we have along the way. But this is not what we find to be the case. For while all other creatures take pleasure in following the order assigned to them by their creator, we take a sullen, perverse and quarrelsome attitude about what we should enjoy. And rather than making it our business to discover the purpose for which God created things for our use, we look for what is wrong with things. We complain about things which should be for our blessing. Man was created to be the lord of the world with all things subject to him, but he has become the slave of what should have been subject to him. He seeks after these things with passion and if they escape him, he is angry and desperate. If he gets them, he over indulges in them and becomes more sick by possessing them than he was by desiring them.

11.   And it will continue to be this way until we learn to keep our desires at home, and not allow them to ramble after things which are out of our reach. God has not put any of us in so barren a place that we do not have things which give us comfort. Let us nourish what we have and we will find it remarkable what improvements we can make. If we do not cultivate our own fields, but instead think only of our neighbors' fields, we may thank ourselves if we starve. This is the result if we are not thankful for what we have. God does not reward us for desiring what we do not have. Our impatience and discontent provokes God.

12.   This is clearly contrary to our best interests and to our duty. We should submit ourselves to the power that made us and not dispute His management of the world or His distribution of things. When we do, we are setting ourselves up

as if we were God. This is more intolerable for Christians than for others. It is a special part of Christian discipline to cheerfully accept our condition: to "know how to be abased, and how to abound, to be full and to be hungry," Philippians 4:12, "to be careful for nothing." Verse 6. Christ does not accept our silly discontent and foolish outcries when we are not hurt. He requires from us more than contentment. He wants us to exult with joy even under heavy pressures, criticism and persecution. "Rejoice ye in that day, and leap for joy," Luke 6:23. And nothing can be more contrary to this than to be always whining and complaining, crying out as the prophet put it, "my leanness, my leanness, woe is me." Isaiah 24:19. Perhaps Moses put it better, "Jesurun waxed fat and kicked." Deuteronomy 32:15.

13.   This quarrelsome attitude is contrary to our interests and our duty, as well as to our peace of mind. It is a sickness of the mind: a continual gnawing and craving without any possibility of being satisfied. It is to the heart what an unsatisfied appetite is to the stomach. As the prophet said, "he shall snatch on the right hand and be hungry, and he shall eat on the left, and not be satisfied." Isaiah 9:20. Where there is much of this strong desire, nothing is nourishing. Everything obtained only excites some new desire. Like a dog, a man may fail to even taste what he eats because of his greedy expectation of the next mouthful. A man with a discontented mind is so intent on his pursuits that he does not appreciate what he acquires. What the prophet says of the covetous is equally true of all discontented persons, "he enlarges his desire as hell, and is as death, and cannot be satisfied." Habakkuk 2:5. And if as Solomon says, "the desire accomplished is sweet to the soul," Proverbs 13:19, it is extremely bitter to be condemned to endless unaccomplished desires. This is the torture which an uncontented spirit provides for itself.

14.   It is madness for people to focus on what is contrary to their own interests and their duty, as well as being contrary to what is easy. You would think that the sensuality of this world would make people oppose anything that was not easy. And yet whatever is their duty, they think to be too laborious; even to spend a few minutes in prayer! "Oh what a weariness is it!" Malachi 1:13. If they so much as miss a meal, they complain that "their knees are weak through fasting," Psalm 109:24. And yet they will wear themselves out with anxiety over their cares and vexations. As the Apostle says, "they pierce themselves through with many sorrows." I Timothy 6:10. People should say about this what Peter said to our Savior, "be it far from thee." Matthew 16:22. Most people are made unhappy not by anything outside them, but by the restlessness and impatience within them.

15.   It is therefore appropriate to try to calm these storms by serious, rational consideration which will show the foolishness of a constant mood of dissatisfaction. It is certain that in truth and logic we can find no basis for this mood, but we can find a great deal to the contrary. In fact, it is so much against reason to cause damage, sin and torment, that if I said nothing more than I already have, it would be enough to show the sin of a mood which cannot be satisfied.

16.   We need not confine our appeal to reason, for it will only tell us what is to our advantage. We must also appeal to what is right. I will insist upon these points. First, God is debtor to no man. Whatever He gives us is by grace only and not because we have any right to it. Second, His bountiful grace is universally dispersed to everyone. Whoever has the very least cannot say he has been poorly dealt with. Third, if we compare the good things we have with our difficulties, the good is far greater. Fourth, we find that the good we have received is far greater than the good we have done, and our afflictions are far less than the sin we have committed. Fifth, since God is the Lord of the universe, it is appropriate for

Him to make such distributions as are good for the whole. Sixth, notwithstanding His universal care, God disposes to each individual what he discerns to be best for that person. Seventh, if we compare our adversities with those of other people, we will always find that which equals or exceeds our own. All of these points are indisputable truths, and any one of them if properly considered, may make us calm and accepting of our situation. And when there are so many such points, it takes a perverse and obstinate attitude to resist them. Taken together with other supportive proof which I will provide, they amount to solid evidence.

SECTION II

Of God's Absolute Sovereignty

1. The first proposition, that God is debtor to no man, is so clear and apparent that it does not require much illustration. He is a free agent and may do as He pleases. He cannot do wrong to anyone because all right exists in Himself. Even the most blind heathens acknowledge this, for they do not consider their idols debtors to themselves, but offer prayers and sacrifices to them. We should acknowledge that God is the source and spring of all things and that in Him, "we live, and move, and have our being." Acts 17:28. It was the free choice of God to make each one of us, and all His subsequent bounties originate only in His own good pleasure. Before we were created, we could put no obligation upon God. And when we began to move, we were only His creatures. Therefore it is indisputable that we owe ourselves to Him. We have no right to claim anything from Him. This is why the Apostle says, "who hath given anything unto Him, and it shall be recompensed unto him again?" Romans 11:35.

2. It is neither prudent nor modest to boldly expect that to which we have no right. And if it is this way with men it must also be so with God who needs nothing from us. As the psalmist says, "our good extends not to Him." Psalm 16:2. God has a fundamental right to what little we may be.

It should then be with great humility that we ask Him for anything, because we can do nothing to deserve it. It is not appropriate for us to have extravagant hopes. Think of the modesty of Mephibosheth, who lost half of what David had given him because of a slanderous accusation, but considered that it had been a gift in the first place, and cheerfully accepted what happened to him, saying "yea, let him take all," 2 Samuel 19:30. We should imitate this rare example, for we also have received all we have as a gift from the King, and as Mephibosheth says in the first part of the verse, "all of my father's house were but dead men before my Lord." May not we say the same? Our entire race was tainted by our first parent. If God had not already owned everything, it would have come to Him by forfeiture because of the fall. Why then do we set our own conditions and expect God to humor us in all our wild demands?

3.   The original rebellion of Adam was to be discontent with the portion God had given to him and to desire that which God had denied him. And this amounts to precisely what the devil proposed: to be like gods. Genesis 3:5. It is an attempt to take the management of the world out of God's hands; to supersede His authority and to give what we want to ourselves. This is madness and insolence, yet it is the true meaning of all the murmuring thoughts we entertain.

4.   Who among us can say "we have made our heart clean?" Proverbs 20:9. It is true that we sometimes make a formal acknowledgment that we receive gifts from God, and it is customary to give thanks at every meal, although even this is being discarded as unfashionable. Such thanks cannot be sincere if during the meal we are grumbling that we do not have what our neighbor has. And God knows that most of our thanksgiving is like this. Indeed we are not as civil to God as we are to men. A common proverb teaches us not to look for blemishes in what is given to us. But with respect to God's gifts, this is exactly what we do, looking for faults

in everything. We act like the buyer Solomon describes: "It is naught, it is naught, saith the buyer." Proverbs 20:14. We absurdly act as if God had an obligation to us, criticizing His gifts to us as if we were angry deities scornfully rejecting whatever does not please our wanton appetites.

5.   If God were to take away all of His blessings which we criticize, what a condition we would be in! And we could not complain if He did so, because it would be a just thing for Him to do. This is what He said to Israel: "I will return, and take away my corn in the time thereof, and my wine in the season thereof, and will recover my wool and my flax." Hosea 2:9. In this verse, He asserts His ownership of these things and reminds us that they are but temporary gifts to us. If He were to remove these things from us, that would not even offend His mercy, for we have treated His gifts with contempt. If any one of us were to give a gift of silver to a poor beggar, and that beggar would grumble because it was not gold, would we not take it back and reserve it for a more worthy person? It is true that our thoughts are not like His thoughts, and our compassion does not measure up to His, and we find in our experience that He is infinitely more longsuffering than we are; yet we learn from the parable of the master and the servant in Matthew 18 that He will proportion His mercy to the extent of our mercy. We have no promise that He will not do so and every reason to expect that He will. God's wisdom causes Him to do nothing in vain. All His bounty is intended to make us happy. When He sees that His purpose is frustrated by our discontent, for what reason should He continue to give us these gifts if we will not be the better because of them?

6.   God is extremely patient, but He takes particular notice not only whether we are diligent, but also whether we are thankful for His blessings or whether we resent them. Men consider ingratitude to be an odious vice. And it is also extremely provoking to God. Consider the words of

our Savior, that from "he that hath not," that is, has not a grateful attitude and who does not value what he has been given, "shall be taken away even that which he hath." Matthew 25:29. We find even a clearer threat made to Israel; "because thou serve not the Lord thy God with gladness and with joyfulness of heart, for the abundance of all things, therefore shalt thou serve thine enemies, whom the Lord God will send among thee, in hunger and in thirst, and in nakedness, and in want of all things." Deuteronomy 28:27-28. This is a sad and dismal reverse action caused wholly by the fact that His people did not have the cheerful gratitude that God expected them to have. And if Israel, God's chosen people, could forfeit His favor by being unthankful, surely none of us can expect otherwise. God loves a cheerful giver, but He also loves a cheerful receiver, who complies with His purpose by being thankful for His gifts. But those with a quarrelsome and unsatisfiable attitude offend God's great bounty by accusing Him of being ungenerous and narrow minded. So it seems that to satisfy His own honor He must cause people to understand Him better by depriving them of things. In this way He teaches them the value of those things in a way they could not learn by the enjoyment of those things.

7. If reason and gratitude are not enough to prevent our sinful murmurings, then let us consider that it is simply unprofitable for us to do so. In fact such murmurings do us actual harm. Let us arm ourselves against this sin by impressing deeply upon our minds that God owes us nothing. Whatever we receive from Him is a gift, not something we have earned. When the Greek philosopher Diogenes was asked which wine was the most pleasing, he answered "that which is drunk at another's expense." Let us remember that whatever good things we have were given to us as free gifts. Whenever we are in an ungrateful mood, and foolishly feel like complaining to God, let us remember the words of the homeowner in the parable, "friend, I do thee no wrong:

Is it not lawful for me to do what I will with mine own?" Matthew 20:15. If God has the right to disburse His gifts however He chooses, then we should not argue with Him. Instead, we should seek and cherish His favor by acts of humble obedience and by giving Him His due honor. All of us would agree that pride and begging do not go together. Instead of that, let us acknowledge God's past mercies to us and our own unworthiness. This was Jacob's method, when he prayed, "I am not worthy of the least of all thy mercies, and of all the truth which thou has shown unto thy servant; for with my staff I passed over this Jordan and now I am become two bands." And after this humble preface, he petitioned God, "deliver me I pray thee from the hand of my brother." Genesis 32:10-11. This is an excellent pattern for prayer, as is shown by its success, and we should follow the example. Indeed, we are utterly destitute of anything in ourselves upon which to base our petitions to God. Instead, our prayers should be based upon what is characteristic of God Himself; that is, His mercy, which He has consistently already shown to us. And God loves to be merciful. We find that both Moses and God Himself recall His past mercies to Israel as the basis for future mercies. Let us therefor come to Him as He himself has taught us, and by gratefully recounting His past mercies, seek for Him to grant us more. This is not hard, if we but seriously remember and consider what we have already received.

SECTION III

Of God's Unlimited Bounty

1. It is a sign of an unworthy nature to write injuries in marble and benefits in dust. As the Roman philosopher Seneca observed, some may avoid doing this with respect to men, but few avoid it with respect to God. And God neither will nor can do us injury. Yet we receive anything which is adverse to us with resentment. And it is those things which we remember, not His great and real blessings to us. So much do we fail to record God's favor to us, that we do not even notice those lasting things which are always before us.

2. Men complain so much that it seems their voices are capable of no other sound. One wants this and another wants that, and all the while everyone of them enjoys a multitude of good things without a single remark. The very breath with which they utter their complaints is a blessing from God and if He were to remove it they would not be able to enjoy anything else which they have or desire. Some have grown so impatient that they despair even of life, because they did not have what they wanted! While this is rare, it shows how depraved the judgment of men can be. A fine jewel is no less valuable because a madman throws it into the fire. The devil, although he is a liar, gave a true statement when he said, "skin for skin, and all that a man hath will

he give for his life." Job 2:4. While perhaps many have in anger been like Jonah and "wished to die," Jonah 4:3, yet it is highly probable that if death were really there, they would want to avoid it. They are like the man in the story who was so weary of his burden of sticks that he threw it down and asked to die, but when death approached him, he accepted its help to pick up his burden again. I appeal to those who have seemed weary of life, and ask whether when suddenly confronted with danger they have not sought to preserve their lives. It is a common saying that as long as there is life, there is hope. What strange reversals in fortune do we see in the history of man! From what despicable beginnings have many arrived at splendid conditions? We have many instances of this both ancient and modern. It is admirable to see what time and industry with God's blessing can bring about. "But there is no work nor device, nor knowledge, nor wisdom in the grave." Ecclesiastes 9:10. We cannot improve when we are gone.

3.   And this is even more true with respect to our spiritual condition. Our life is "the day wherein we are to work," John 9:4, that is, to work out our salvation. But "when the night comes," that is, when death overtakes us, "no man can work." Consider how much of the day we waste. Or even worse, we have been busy doing the wrong things, so that we have to spend our time fixing what we have done. And it may take a lot of time to do so. Our works may be like a "spider's web," Isaiah 59:5, which cannot quickly be undone. Bad habits lie too deep to be swept away. It is not easy to convince ourselves to be rid of them. It may take a difficult, serious and long course of action before we are free of them. They are not like the Centurion's servants. They may come when we bid them but they will not go. They must be expelled by force and by slow degrees. We must fight for every inch of ground we gain from them. God did not give the Israelites victory over Canaan all at once. And neither does He give us quick and easy victory over sin. Not only do we need to

end bad habits, but we also need to acquire good habits. We cannot enter the marriage chamber with empty lamps. Matthew 25:10. "We must add to our faith virtue, and to virtue knowledge, and to knowledge temperance, etc." 2 Peter 1:5. No link must be missing in that sacred chain. But as the same Apostle also says, we must "be holy in all manner of conversation." I Peter 1:15.

4. Now I ask the reader to seriously consider whether such good habits and disciplines have been established in him. If so, he is a happy man and has no outside needs, for he that is fed with manna must be perverse indeed if he murmurs for a belly full of "leeks and onions." Numbers 11:15. On the contrary, he owes infinite thanks to God who gave him the time on this earth to develop such a spiritual life. Even the best of us are not so innocent that they cannot remember times of sin when it would have been dreadful to have been taken away. But how comprehensive and bountiful a mercy has their life been to them, which has carried eternity in its womb and qualified them for Heaven. And they should not look upon this merely as a past blessing, but in the present and future as well, for it both confirms and advances their reward. God may glorify Himself by using them in His service, which is both the greatest honor and the greatest satisfaction to a good heart. One should not so long for his reward that he grows impatient of his present duty. He that loves God finds blessing in serving Him. In this way life itself is a mercy to a godly man, and obligates him to be contented and thankful.

5. If a man cannot give this good account of his life, but is aware of his many faults, that does not lessen his obligation to God, who intended him to live better. It is merely his own fault. In fact, the worse a man's life has been, the greater the mercy of God that his pattern of life has not become irreversible; that God has not ended his earthly life and the possibility of Heaven as well. But God affords him "yet a longer

day, if yet he will hear His voice." Psalm 95:7. This long suffering is one of the greatest signs of God's goodness. As the Apostle says, "the riches of His goodness and long suffering and forbearance." Romans 2:4. We commonly acknowledge this only when we have worn it out and can no longer take advantage of it. How precious to a gasping, despairing soul, is a small parcel of the time he used to squander! Oh that men would value time this much when they still had use of it, and that they would be more thankful for it, "accounting that the long suffering of the Lord is salvation." 2 Peter 3:15.

6. If men correctly added up the true benefits in life, they would see that they are far greater than all the struggles and anxiety of it. It is shameful that we spend our breath in sighs and complaints, when that very breath was given to us for a more noble purpose. If we used our breath as God intended, it would overcome our complaints, and we would acknowledge that God has been kind to us, even though we may live a humble life. "Our life is given us for a prey." Jeremiah 45:5. He that has still great work to do in his life cannot afford to waste time upon regrets, since his entire stock of time is barely enough to make up for his past neglect of eternal concerns. Even if we had no outward comforts in this life and faced only continual problems, yet this one blessing of life would outweigh them all and render our murmurings inexcusable.

7. But God has not put any of us to the ultimate test. He has given no one such complete calamity that he does not also have some outward comforts. This must be acknowledged if we consider how many blessings are shared by all of mankind. The four elements, fire, water, air and earth, supply our basic needs. And the sun, moon and stars, as Moses tells us, are by "God divided to all nations under the whole Heaven." Deuteronomy 4:19. Those resplendent bodies give their light and influence to everyone. The sun shines as brightly on the poor cottage as it does on the most magnificent palace. And

the stars shine as much for him that is "behind the mill, as for him that sits on the throne." Exodus 11:5. The celestial lights are every man's treasure and no man's in particular, which shows us that our tendency to apportion ownership "defends not from above." James 3:15.

8. And these universal blessings make no distinction between the ranks and degrees of men, or of their virtues. As our Savior tells us, "God causes His sun to rise on the good and on the evil, and sends rain on the just and the unjust." Matthew 5:45. The animals which serve us do so equally to the rich and the poor. The horse draws a poor man's plough as tamely as a rich man's chariot, and a beggar's dog follows him as faithfully as the pampered lap dogs of the nicest ladies. The sheep obey a poor shepherd as well as the daughters of the wealthy Laban, Genesis 29:9, or of Jethro, a prince, Exodus 2:16, and as willingly yield their wool to clothe Lazarus, as to make purple robes for Dives. So also vegetables feed rich and poor alike. The fruits refresh and the flowers delight the poor man as well as the rich.

9. But I see that some will object to this, and say that these universal privileges are insignificant, because not every man has them to use. My answer is that many of these things cannot be monopolized. The worst oppressor cannot lock up the sun. "He that lays house to house, and land to land, till there be no place," Isaiah 5:8, cannot enclose the air. And this may be said of many things. There are many blessings which continue to be the universal right of mankind.

10. It is not to be denied that there is a great difference in the manner in which God has dispensed various things; as great as Nathan's parable describes when he speaks of the numerous flocks of the rich man and the "single ewe lamb of the poor" man. 2 Samuel 12:2. But there are few who are so poor that they cannot by one means or another obtain what is necessary for life. If such things are not acquired by birth right and inheritance, they may be obtained by labor and

industry, which is in many ways better. Such persons might not have "Sodom's fullness of bread," or its "abundance of idleness," Ezekiel 16:49, or what Agur wished for, "food convenient." Proverbs 30:8. And if they fold their hands upon their stomachs like Solomon's sluggard, they will not plow "by reason of the cold," and therefore "they may beg in harvest and have nothing." Proverbs 10:14, then it is clear that they are the authors of their own circumstances. Indeed, for such men of lazy, careless natures, it is hard to say what degree of God's bounty could keep them from want. We often see fortune dissipated by negligence and waste. If men choose to be idle, they ought not to accuse God, but themselves if they are poor.

11. It is true that some people are unable to work because of age, sickness or disability. And this is the worst type of poverty. Yet God has provided for these persons also by assigning them to the rich. They are like God's representatives in that He has given them authority to demand relief in His name and on his account. And while it is true that even this authority will not prevail upon many of the rich to open their purses, yet even in this age of frozen charity, there are still some who remember upon what terms they received their wealth and use it properly. And while this is not as large a portion of them as we would hope for, yet everywhere there are some who are like "cities of refuge" in the land, Deuteronomy 19:2, to which the distressed poor may flee for relief. And I think I may say that between government programs and private charity, there are not many who still need the most basic necessities. Remember that the apostle Paul considered those necessities to be only food and clothing, and considered them enough with which to be content. I Timothy 6:8. I do not say this to lessen any man's compassion for the poor, for however much they give, I wish as Joab did to David, that the Lord would increase it one hundred fold. 2 Samuel 24:3. I only suggest this as evidence of what I am trying to prove, that no one is so predestined by God

to such desperate circumstances, that he does not share in God's provision. Therefore no one should murmur, for even the most indigent still receives blessings from God.

12.   But the number of people in such a condition is few compared to those in a higher position. For between the lowest and the highest circumstances, there are many intermediate degrees, in which people have not only the necessities but also comforts in life. They have not only food and clothing, but also their choice of days to work or rest and their choice of food and clothing. And he that is but one step above beggary has more than he needs, and to every degree to which he rises, he becomes subject to vanity and excess. Among those who rise gradually, some have so many luxuries that they do not know what to do with them. How many there are who have so satisfied their desires that they search for some other pleasure to indulge in and are distressed about what to do with their abundance.

13.   While surely these very people cannot deny that they have received good things, generally they are the most discontented. This clearly demonstrates that their complaints do not arise from any defect in God's bounty, but from a defect in their own attitudes. It is easier to cure hunger than to cure the sickness of an overfed stomach. The discontent of the poor is more easily resolved than the discontent of the rich. The very indigence of the poor has lessened his desires, and has taught him not to seek much beyond what is truly necessary. But he who by continually having all he wants finds that his desires are stretched and extended, is not capable of such satisfaction. He does not know what to seek next. He thinks himself miserable because he does not know what will make him happy. Yet this is the condition which people envy and aspire to! Every man thinks he will be happy if there remains nothing that he does not have. He does not know that this would torment him. No one should think that contentment is found in continually chasing after

things. He is most likely to find contentment at home if he thinks about those blessings which God has put within his reach, and of which every man has a fair portion.

14. Besides those external things, of which the poor have some, those in the middle a great deal and the rich too much, man is a principality in and of himself. He has within him so much evidence of his maker's power and goodness, that he needs no external thing to be happy. If he knew the right way to value himself, he would appreciate that even the least part of himself, his body, is a remarkable example of God's workmanship. As the psalmist says, "he is fearfully and wonderfully made." It is astonishing to consider the symmetry of parts from which this beautiful fabric of the body is made. And these parts are not only for show, but for use. Every part is given a particular ability so that it may serve the whole, and no part is unnecessary. The most useful parts are capable of covering for another part if it is injured. And this is an example of the bounty of the Creator. After Galen, the Roman physician, had attempted to prevent himself and those of his profession from even thinking about God, he considered the human body; how every part interacts and how the strength, agility and movement greatly surpass any machine; and he broke forth in praise for the Creator. Consider also the wonder of our senses; those "five operations of the Lord," as the son of Syrach rightly calls them. By them we may experience the world. What would be the beauty of the universe if we could not see it? Or what would be the greatest music if we could not hear it? And almost everyone has been given these operational senses, although because of our tendency to undervalue them, God has sometimes taken them away in order to show us their true worth.

15. God has also provided much refreshment for our bodies. He has given us sleep and allowed us sufficient time for it. Yet who remembers to be thankful for the mercy of sleep when he lies down or when he rises refreshed? It is only when our

rest is interrupted by an anxious mind or bodily pain that we consider that it is "God who gives His beloved sleep," Psalm 127:2, and remember what a blessing it is. It is the same way with our health, our strength and everything else. We don't think about it when we have it, but impatiently desire it when we do not. We should not complain that God's hand is too short towards us when we commonly enjoy these mercies for many years but miss them so much if they are withdrawn for a few hours. Indeed, there is no greater example of human depravity than our senseless contempt of God's blessings just because they are customary. In fact, for this reason we should prize them even more. If a man were to give me one hundred dollars on one occasion, I would appreciate it, but if it were my annual revenue, I would not. God loses the thanksgiving to which He is due because He multiplies His favor to us. His blessings grow invisible just because they are always before us.

16. But the body which we may enjoy is but the least part of God's bounty. It is merely a suitable container for that jewel of inestimable value which God has placed in it, the soul, which is the purpose for which the body was made. The soul is a spark of divinity in which God accomplished His design of "making man in His own image." Genesis 1:26. It is not possible to list here all the wonders of the soul. Its mere intellectual power is remarkable. Yet it is a mystery to itself. The most simple man knows that he has the powers of imagination, apprehension, memory and reflection, yet the most learned man cannot determine how these powers operate. It is enough to us to know that we have them and to consider the wonderful uses for them; one of the most important of which is a thankful reflection on the goodness of God who gave them. He might have made us as insensible as a stone or as a lesser type of animal. But He gave us the highest position among all of the visible creatures and gave us "dominion over the works of His hands." Psalm 8:6. And He gave us the faculty of reason with which to manage

that sovereignty, without which we would have been mere brutes.

17. The soul should be considered in an even higher light. It is immortal and has the capacity for eternal happiness. And it is this aspect which reflects God Himself, whose happiness is part of His very being. This capacity is the highest part of human beings, and it is universal. While men may differ in many ways, in this they are equal. The poor beggar at the gate has a soul as capable of eternal happiness as does he whose crumbs he begs for; and he may be better prepared for it, as the parable of the shrewd manager illustrates. Luke 16:11. The dignities of the earth are the prize of the rich and the noble, yet heaven is as easily attained from a dung hill as from a throne. An honest simplicity is all that is needed to bring us there. Not only has God designed for us to have such a glorious end, but He entirely on His own has done what is necessary to secure it for us, by sending His Son to lead the way and His Spirit to quicken us. And although the opportunity is universal, it is attained only by those who make up the true church. They have a particular obligation, as those singled out from the rest of the world, to be the more thankful for it. As the heathen philosophers acknowledged that they were born Greeks and not barbarians, the advantages of being a Christian are infinitely more to be celebrated. The Apostle often applauded this glorious privilege which makes us "fellow citizens with the saints, and of the household of God." Ephesians 3:19. And greater still to "the adoption of sons," Galatians 3:19, and "heirs also of God, and joint heirs with Christ." Romans 8:17. What ambition could be so greedy that this will not satisfy it? Yet this is the condition which we share; the birth right of regeneration, if we do not degrade ourselves and like Esau sell our title for some base thing.

18. Every man should ask himself as did Jonadab to Amon, 2 Samuel 13:4, "why art thou, being the king's son, thus lean

from day to day?" Why should a person who has been adopted by the King of Kings languish and complain? What is there under the sun worthy of his notice, much less his desires, when he has a Kingdom above it? If we really understood this, it would not be possible for us to so impatiently seek after petty worldly interests and to be so upset when we do not get them. In what an unworthy manner do we bear the name of Christians when the faith which carried our forefathers through the most fiery trials cannot support us when we are disappointed by not getting those extravagant things which we desire? They had such "respect to the recompence of the reward," Hebrews 11:26, that they cheerfully exposed themselves to poverty, theft, torture and death. Yet the same hope does not produce in us patience when we suffer the very smallest loss in the value of our possessions. Is heaven less valuable or earth more so than it was then? Surely not, but it is we who have become infatuated with worldly wealth. We have for so long succumbed to the rivalry of the hand maid, that the mistress, like Sarah, appears despicable. Like Jonah we sit and pout when the gourd withers, and do not consider that God has provided for us a better shelter, "a building of God eternal in the heavens," 2 Corinthians 5:1. No worldly loss is so great that this expectation cannot lift us up. Even if we were in Job's condition, sitting upon a dung hill and scraping ourselves with a piece of broken pottery, yet as long as we could say with him, "our redeemer liveth," Job 19:25, we have all reason to also say with him, "blessed be the name of the Lord." Job 1:21. What madness it is to allow ourselves to be pierced and wounded by every adversity, when we have an impenetrable armor! How ungrateful it is to the goodness of God to not allow He Himself to overcome our trivial secular satisfactions. He may again make that accusation against us which we find in the prophet, "a goodly price that I was valued at by them." Zechariah 11:13.

19.   Remember that Christ said that he "that loves father or mother, son or daughter more than Him, is not worthy of Him." Matthew 10:37. Our love, our joy and our passions are coincident with one another. Whatever gives us more joy than He Himself, it may be presumed that we love better than Him. If He cannot bear the competition of our love for lesser things, how will he suffer our vanities and our childish wanton appetites? And yet those are the things we so impatiently demand. Of all the discontents of mankind caused by great calamities, there are many more that arise merely out of the irregularity of our own desires.

20.   We may therefore conclude as the prophet said, that "God hath not been to us a wilderness, a land of darkness," Jeremiah 2:31, but has graciously dispensed to us all that we need. The examples here given are only what is common to the majority of people. But how many volumes could be written if every one of us were to record his own experiences of mercy? It would be no exaggeration to say as did John, "that even the world itself could not contain the books which should be written." John 22:25. God knows that our memories are frail and our observations slight. Yet even without all that has been forgotten, what a great list each of us could recall of God's bounty to us and protection of us, not to mention His patient forbearance of our sins and weaknesses. And certainly it was not intended that we should fail to notice these things. As the psalmist tells us, "the Lord has so done His marvelous works that they ought to be had in remembrance." Psalm 111:4. Let every man then make it his daily discipline to recount to himself the wonders which God has done for all people, and for himself in particular. When the Israelites murmured in their bondage, Pharoah attributed it to their idleness and gave them more work to do. While this was inhumane tyranny on his part, yet we may apply the principle with fairness and success to ourselves. When we find ourselves complaining about our present condition, let us set ourselves to work. Let us

make it our task to remember the many instances of God's mercy. If we do this with sincerity, we will soon find that our murmurings will stop. We will remember them with shame when we perceive all the evidence of God's goodness to us. For when we add up all our little grievances and examine all our wants, we will find them disproportionate to our comforts and our receipts.

SECTION IV

Of the Surplus of our Enjoyment above our Suffering

1. To have a proper understanding of our enjoyment and our suffering, three things must be considered. The first is the number of them. The second is their significance. And the third is how long they remain. For it is in proportion to these three considerations that we may judge how good or how evil our experiences may be. We should therefor consider our blessings and our calamities in these three respects.

2. As to the number of things which we may enjoy, let us remember that the mercies of God are the source of all good, and are laid out in scripture in grand superlatives. They are "multitude," Psalm 102:20, "plenteous redemption," Psalm 130:7, "as high as the Heaven," Psalm 130:11, "He fills all living things with plenteousness," Psalm 145:16. In fact, His mercies cannot be numbered, but stretch to infinity. They are best represented as God did to Abraham, when He showed him how numerous would be his posterity by showing him the stars. Genesis 15:5. Even if we received but one mercy per minute, the number would be very high, but how can we count them when every minute has more than we can number? For not only do we have the mercies mentioned in the last section, but He gives us a bounty of

new mercies continuously. We are each one of us made up of so many parts, have such a variety of interests, spiritual, temporal, public and private, for ourselves, our friends and our families, that it is not just some general blessing that keeps all these secure. We are like a vast building, which costs as much to maintain as to erect. And indeed, considering the corruptibleness of our materials, our preservation is no less an act of God's great power than was our creation; perhaps greater. For our original clay was in the hands of the Potter to make what He pleased, but now we are subject to decay. Without the many things we need to maintain us, we would return to the dust. Not only this, but we are subject to forces which may attack us. The very air which refreshes us may also starve and freeze us. That which warms and comforts us has the power to consume us. Even the food which nourishes us may choke or stifle us. There is in fact nothing which serves us which may not also ruin us. Why is it that we so often find good in these things and so rarely harm in them? It is the active and tireless providence of God which brings forth the better properties of these things for our use, and restrains the worst properties for our security. He watches over every person and every concern of every person. How amazing it is to contemplate this. If the mere ebbing and flowing of the sea put the philosopher into such ecstasy that he threw himself into it because he could not comprehend the inscrutable cause of it, then in what perpetual rapture of admiration should we be in, since we have every minute, both within us and about us, more and greater wonders than this? And these wonders work in our favor when we deserve destruction.

3. Our danger from that which is visible is small when compared to those dangers which we face from the spirits of darkness. "We wrestle not only with flesh and blood, but with principalities and powers, with spiritual wickedness, etc." Ephesians 6:12. So great is the enmity between the serpent and the seed of the woman, that he looks for every

opportunity to gain an advantage over us, not only with respect to our souls, but also our bodies, our possessions and everything about which we are concerned. Not only did he afflict Job's soul by the wicked things his wife said to him, but he also afflicted his body with boils and sores, and destroyed his property, his children and his view of himself. Job 1. And can we think that his hatred to us has been used up? No, he surely wants to cause as much harm to mankind as ever. And we would see the full effects of this, were it not that the same power which let him loose to attack Job also restrains him for our safety. Even if the evil one had power merely to frighten us but not to harm us, that alone would be more than we could bear. Yet he would do all this and more if God did not chain up this "old dragon." Revelation 20. But God has set up His angels as a guard around us. As the Apostle says, "that they are all ministering spirits, sent forth to minister for them, who shall be heirs of salvation." Hebrews 1:14. If any one of us were to count up his many concerns and dangers, they would not measure up to those mercies which preserve and protect us. As the psalmist said, "they are more than I am able to express." Psalm 40:7.

4.   I challenge the most miserable or the most argumentative man to produce evidence that his complaints equal his causes for thanksgiving. He that has suffered the greatest calamities will find that they simply do not measure up to the number of his blessings. The difference between them is greater than that of the armies of Ahab and Benhadad, I Kings 20:27, where the one was like "two little flocks of kids, the other filled the country." God has told us that He "afflicts not willingly, nor grieves the children of men," Lamentations 3:33. On the contrary, He "delighteth in mercy," Micah 7:18. Judge for yourself what God is most likely to do, that which He does with regret and reluctance, or that which He does with pleasure and delight. But we do not need to infer that which we see by our own experience. Every one of us should every night consider his many concerns and how

God has that day preserved him, and consider that each such preservation is a new blessing. If we begin by considering our spiritual condition, we will remember that we are not innocent and that even in our sin, God has preserved us with inward checks and admonitions and with outward restraints. And if we have sinned despite these fences, that does not lessen the mercy of God who guarded us, but illustrates His goodness, that even though we have quenched His Spirit, yet He continues in His influence over us. Even he who has the most deplorably violated his own integrity, must confess that it was God's purpose to preserve that integrity, and that He provided sufficient aids which would have enabled him to do so. We are far less likely to do this with respect to worldly concerns than we are with respect to our spiritual concerns. Let us consider each night what possessions we have lost that day and we will most likely agree with the account given by the Israelite officers of their men after the slaughter of the "Midianites; that he hath not lost one." Numbers 31:39. And if we do suffer a loss, yet we find that many more good things have been preserved. A man may lose part of his estate, yet it is likely that more is preserved than lost. And if he should lose his entire estate, if he still has his limbs, his senses, his friends and many other things, he may say as the disciples did of the loaves, "what is this among so many?" Matthew 14:7. When the Greek philosopher Aristippus was consoled upon the loss of a farm, he replied to the one who was consoling him, "you have one field and I have three left. Should I not console you?" This teaches us that a man should not measure what he loses but what he has left. It is wise to consider as Elijah said, that there are "more with us than against us," 2 Kings 6:16, and that our enjoyments are greater than our sufferings, and God's acts of grace far out-number His acts of severity.

5.   And as the number of God's blessings and our enjoyment of them is far greater than our sufferings, so also do they outweigh them. The mercies we receive from God are of the

greatest importance, and while they do involve substantial and solid goods, far greater are those which concern our eternal estate. These are so firmly fixed on us, that unless we voluntarily quit our claim to them, it is not in the power of men or devils to defeat us. Light bodies are easily blown away by every gust of wind, but we have this "weight of glory," as the Apostle put it, 2 Corinthians 4:7, which continues firm and stable against all types of storms, like the "shadow of a great rock in a weary land," Isaiah 32:2. The dark and hazy view which we have of this may yet serve to refresh us in our pilgrimage, and remind us that all those formidable calamities of this life do not compare to the hope of our calling, those "riches of the glory of our inheritance," Ephesians 3:16. The heaviest and the most pressing of our afflictions are, when compared to this, but "small dust of the balance." Ephesians 4:14. So, if we stopped our discussion here we have already sufficient evidence that God has given us an abundant counter balance to our suffering.

6.   If anyone is so poor that he can find no evidence of God's fatherly care for him, then let him consider this one thing. We read that Abraham gave no gifts to Isaac, but that he did give gifts to the sons of his concubines. Genesis 25:6. It would have been false for Isaac to have considered himself neglected because of what was reserved for him. And it is the same for us. We should not consider God unkind to us because we are poor, when we have such an eternal inheritance. But surely "God does not leave Himself without witness," Acts 14:17, even in earthly matters. There is no man breathing who does not have some blessings both on his left and on his right. And except for a few persons in whose lives God is bringing hardships for a specific purpose in which to glorify Himself, there is no one who does not enjoy greater comforts in life than any he may be without. I mean that which is really greater, although it may not presently appear to be so. In health, for example, a man may suffer harm to one part of his body, and yet the rest of his body is well. We

are generally more healthy than ill. And while some may lose a limb or a sense, yet most keep them all their lives. And it often pleases God to improve our use of one thing to compensate for the loss of another. We have seen those without hands learn to do remarkable things with their feet. And we have seen those who are blind develop a greater internal light and gain a more vigorous and active intellect because they are not distracted by visible objects.

7. It is the same with respect to wealth. It is true that he who is forced to earn his daily bread by the sweat of his brow cannot have those delicacies which rich men enjoy, yet his very labor helps him to have a far greater enjoyment of what he has. His very hunger makes his bread taste better than those rich foods which the overfed cannot really enjoy. As Solomon said, "the full soul loathes the honey comb, but to the hungry soul, every bitter thing is sweet." Proverbs 27:7. The poor man cannot "indeed stretch himself upon his bed of ivory," Amos 6:4, yet he sleeps more soundly than those who can. The wise man tells us, as does our experience, that "the sleep of a laboring man is sweet." Ecclesiastes 5:12. He who is not dressed in fine clothing also does not have the care of obtaining it, nor the concern about always having the latest fashion or the many other anxieties which vanity produces. But he does have the proper and genuine use of clothing, to keep him warm and covered. And this is what the wise men of the world have chosen voluntarily. In addition to this, his very necessities rescue him from idleness and all its temptations. This is a great advantage, for a rich man must be his own task master, while a poor man's very need is his. This need of the rich for self-control is greater than the need of the poor, who is happy in comparison and still has better things than he actually needs.

8. If we consider the issue of reputation, we will find the same principles to apply. If a person is famous for some great achievement, he becomes highly visible, and both his good

qualities and his faults are on display. With human nature being what it is, it is probable that his faults will be more noticeable than any good he has done; because envy causes people to focus on the faults. Therefore, a good, quiet security is better. It does not lead to fame, but it also does not lead to infamy. He that can maintain the reputation of a sober integrity within his own private sphere should not envy those whose triumphs are widely noticed, for their fame is likely to take a bitter turn in the end. But some will say that even the humble may suffer a bad reputation. To this, I ask whether it is just or unjust. If it is just, then it does not relate to our subject matter, for we are considering only those afflictions which are brought about by God's design. I have not suggested that we could not voluntarily give up God's blessings to us. But if we suffer unjust criticism, then it is likely that it comes only from men of ill will, and not from those who make fair judgments. And surely the judgment of good men should outweigh the criticism of others. Viewed in this way, we may actually take pleasure in such criticism. The Greek philosopher Socrates was troubled when people commended him and asked himself what he had done wrong. And surely a Christian has better reason to be pleased when he is reviled, for those criticisms are his defense against the "woe" pronounce to those "whom all men speak well of." Luke 6:26. But sometimes even good men are seduced by the world and believe false reports. And while this is a difficult trial for the injured person, yet it is almost never a universal viewpoint. It is rare for any innocent person to suffer such a bad reputation that there is no opportunity to clear it up; and when it is, their reputation is likely to be the better for it. But even if this does not happen, we may still appeal to that great judge who sees us with more pleasure when we suffer the unjust criticism of men, for then not only His justice but also His pity is shown to us. God declares Himself to be the refuge of the oppressed. When we suffer unjustly we become particular objects of

His care and compassion, and He can "make our righteousness as clear as the light," Psalm 37:6, if He chooses to do so. But even if He does not, it should be comfort enough for us to know that He approves of us. This was Elkanah's question to Hannah, in an attempt to console her; "am I not better to thee than ten sons?" I Samuel 1:8. And we may say the same of God's approval, that it is better than ten thousand compliments from men. The very remembrance and appreciation of God's approval is the sweetest in the midst of the most harsh accusations of men. So we see that in the matter of reputation, God has provided a defense and even the "waters of Marah," Exodus 15:23, may be rendered not only wholesome, but pleasant also.

9.   I have discussed the three most general concerns of human life, the body, possessions and reputation. Most of the afflictions which we personally experience fall into one of these three categories. But no one lives alone in this world, and we may all suffer as a result of what happens to those we love; and this may be the more painful. But in this also God provides help to us, if we will take notice of it. Most of us have more than one friend, and if death takes one away, others may be found. We only have one set of parents, yet we may have friends who are as helpful to us as they were. Indeed this is some of the greatest evidence of God's provision. "He that is able out of stones to raise up children to Abraham," Matthew 3:9, does often provide friends for those who need them. Sometimes we lose our friends because they withdraw their kindness, which is the heart of friendship. If this happens because of what we ourselves have done, then we cannot blame either them or God. We cannot rationally expect God to provide what we need when we do harm to ourselves. But when our friends are unkind without provocation, then the reason may be found in God's intervening for a purpose. For He will take up "those whom father and mother forsake," Psalm 27:10. We often see His care shown through the compassion of other friends

and relatives, or even strangers. Sometimes God is at work through the inhuman actions of others. Consider that the barbarity and hatred of Joseph's brothers was the first step towards his dominion over Egypt. And many have observed that in families, often the least appreciated child excels over the darling.

10. We may also suffer because of calamities which overtake our friends; sometimes more than if it had happened to us. When this happens, we should remember that they are subject to the same things we are, and that God may lift their burdens as well. So what we have said about our own suffering applies to them as well. We are better friends if we help them to understand this, than if we merely take their sorrows as our own.

11. The greatest sorrow we may draw from our friends is that sorrow which is caused by their sin. Yet even this "valley of Achor is not without a door of hope," Hosea 2:15. A person may be brought back from his sin, as many have been. So long as God continues life, we ought not to give up hope or stop our efforts. Few who carry the burden of the sin of a friend do not also find something in the balance to lighten that burden. This is much the same as the experience of a parent, who may have one bad child but several good ones, and who may appreciate them all the more because of the struggles caused by the one. But if anyone is so unhappy as to have many children who are acting badly, and "all to consume his eyes, and to grieve his heart," 1 Samuel 2:33, it may be wise to consider how much he himself has contributed to their behavior, either by too much fond indulgence or too careless an education; or worst of all by his own bad example. And if he finds this to be the case, he should not so much seek solace from friends as to seek pardon for his sin. And when he has made his own life right with God, he may have a better hope that God may reform the lives of his children. Until that happens, he may consider the problems

might well have been satisfied with the whole Kingdom of Israel had not Naboth's poor plot of land caught his eye. Yet so raving were his desires for it that he despised all the glory of being the king. A man will eat no bread until he has found a salad to go with it. 1 Kings 21:2. How many are there these days whose clothes fit uneasy if they see another wearing something more fancy, or whose food loses its taste because another has a rare delicacy. In a word, we make other people's excesses the standard of our own happiness.

15. Our appetites are not only excited by outward objects, but they are also caused and increased by the lusts within us. The proud man longs for adoration, and without it nothing can please him. Haman could not be satisfied by all the sensualities of the Persian court because a poor despicable Jew would not give him honor. Esther 5:13. The lustful are so impatient in pursuing their designs that they fret like Amnon, who could only recover his health by violating his sister's honor. 2 Samuel 13:14. Those who seek revenge thirst for the blood of their enemies, like Absalom, who could not be satisfied except to slaughter his brother. 2 Samuel 13:22. Every one of our passions tortures us until they have obtained their design. And when they do, the very emptiness of the accomplishment drives them to new pursuits. Between the impetuousness of our desires and the emptiness of our enjoyment, we "disquiet ourselves in vain." Psalm 39:7. With such cruel taskmasters, is it any wonder that we groan under our burdens! If we live this way, we have as angry an impatience as did Rachel for children, when she said, "give me them or I die." Genesis 30:1. No wonder then that we complain of our disappointments, for in the very success there is defeat. We merely exchange the pain of our empty stomach for the nausea of an overfilled stomach. Those who live this way condemn themselves to perpetual restlessness. Like mutineers, they seek to control the ship but do not know which way to go. If they had the power to gain everythi· which they desired, they would still be lost.

16.   How unjustly do they accuse God of not being generous just because His gifts do not conform to their moods? He has made them to be reasonable creatures and has provided them blessings proportionate to their nature. If they have wild, irrational expectations, they will find that neither His wisdom nor His goodness was designed to satisfy those expectations. God's gifts are real and solid. They do not correspond to imaginary wants. If we create imaginary wants, why not also create imaginary satisfactions for them? That would be the merrier frenzy of the two! It would be like the mad Athenian who thought that all the ships which came into the harbor belonged to him. Like Ixion, from Greek mythology, it would be better to have our arms filled with clouds, than to beat our breasts, being tormented by desires which cannot be satisfied. Yet this is the condition which men voluntarily subject themselves to, and then quarrel with God because they will not allow themselves to be happy. Surely their very complaints show both the justice and the kindness of God, and that He has given them the necessary accommodations for life. For if they had real need, they would not even be sensible of their wants. He that is at ease will feel the bite of a flea, but he that is in real pain would never feel it. And if God were to cause these nice people to feel the true destitution of necessity, their regrets over not having the superfluous things they desire would be overwhelmed. How deplorable it is that we are the poorer for all God's bounty, and that those to whom He has opened His hand the widest, should open their mouths in outcries and murmurs. I think that I may say that those who are the most removed from want are also the farthest from contentment. They do not take notice of the real substantial blessings which they enjoy. They leave these (like the ninety-nine sheep in the wilderness) forgotten and neglected, to seek after some fugitive satisfaction, which like a shadow flies the faster away the more they run after it.

17. How very much I desire that God would recall them from this unprofitable chase: that instead of crying, "give, give," Proverbs 30:5, they would say with the psalmist, "what shall I render to the Lord for all the benefits He hath done unto me?" Psalm 116:12. Let them count how many things of inestimable value they have received by His mercy, and let them see how they would have fared if God had brought His justice upon them. If they were to do this impartially, I have no doubt that they would find the means to control their mutinous attitudes, and would join me in confessing that their good things greatly outweigh the bad.

18. If we now consider how long our experiences endure, we shall also find a great difference. Consider the testimony of the psalmist, who said, "His mercies endure forever," Psalm 136, whereas His wrath "endures but the twinkling of an eye." Psalm 30:5. And God characterizes His own acts of severity as His "strange work." Isaiah 28:21, which He resorts to only upon special circumstances. But His mercies "are renewed every morning." Lamentations 3:23. There is no doubt that each of us would affirm that this has been our experience. We have many of the most necessary comforts of life every day, and many have lived in such consistent affluence that they have never known a real need. And those who have not had such blessings, nevertheless experience the universal refreshments of nature. We eat and drink, we sleep and play, all in a continuous circle, nearly as constant as the rising and setting of the sun. And while God may sometimes cause this cycle to be interrupted, it is usually for a short time; a brief pause in the customary benefits which He allots to us. Who among us can claim that his afflictions have been as constant as his blessings? We may miss a few nights sleep, but what is that in a year or a lifetime? We may sometimes have to wait to eat, but usually we do not. That which is most useful is rarely interrupted. And for many, their luxuries are as consistent as their necessities. Most of our uneasiness comes either from our own sin or our

unwarranted desires. Uneasiness brought by God does not last long. Yet if one were to judge by the complaints of men, he would think that the reverse was true, and that our good things were as Job says, "swifter than a weavers shuttle," Job 7:6, and our bad things like "Gehazy's leprosy, cleave inseparable to us." 2 Kings 5:27.

19.   The truth is that we do not allow ourselves to enjoy times of peace, because even when a calamity has gone, we keep it in our minds, telling ourselves that it could return again. When we are healthy, we worry about being sick. It is a strange and stupid folly to always look towards the illusion of an evil which we think might happen. Does any man or beast desire to keep a bad taste in the mouth? Yet many people allow themselves to remain embittered by imaginary sufferings. Not only do we frighten ourselves with the memory of past calamities, but we imagine new ones which we think might occur. This is common to people with a jealous nature who are always raising alarms. A suspicious man looks on everybody with dread. One man fears for his fortune, another for his reputation, a third for his life; while the only evil design against them is that which they themselves imagine. It is their own unfounded fear and jealousy which puts them in a state of hostility with the world. And it is this which often causes the very thing which they feared. It is not unusual for people to incur real problems in an attempt to avoid imaginary ones. This, itself becomes a real state of calamity, and it is likely that such people will experience no truce from this kind of war. We may say, as did the prophet to the house of Jacob, "is the Spirit of God strained? Are these His doings?" Micah 2:7. It is not the hand of God which lies heavy upon such people, but their own. And so this does not alter our observation that God's blessings are of a longer duration and keep a more steady course, than His punishments. The majority of people have good things, far greater in number, weight and constancy, than the bad things they

may experience; if we consider only what is real and not what we imagine.

20.   Is it not reasonable that we should think more about the pleasant things which God gives rather than the hard things? And this is especially so since the pleasant things are far better for our consideration and much more numerous. Why should we choose to look upon the fading spectacles of human frailty or misfortune as though through a magnifying glass, and turn our eyes away from that which is good? Yet this is too often what we do. How carefully we examine everything that goes wrong, and how often do we speak about those things. While we do this, the whole current of prosperity glides by us without notice. Like children, we pick at our sores until they bleed. We even pretend we have sores just so that we can complain. Why then would we expect God to concern Himself with healing such sores? Instead, in God's ordinary providence there is no cure for such people, unless it comes by sending real and substantial wounds. They create this dilemma; to continue tormenting themselves or to endure God's discipline. The best way to prevent all of this is to have a just and grateful sense of God's mercies, which we will the more appreciate if we consider our own demerits.

SECTION V

Of Our Demerit towards God

1. It is a common fault of our nature that we are partial to ourselves. Our expectations are based more upon what we desire than upon what we deserve. And this is evident in how we relate to others. We often "look to reap where we have not sowed." Matthew 25:25. We expect benefits that we have not earned. Yet we are not so unreasonable in our law or our commerce, where we expect fair transactions. In our dealings with God, however, we forget this sense of fairness and have vast expectations, for which we give little in return. We act as if God were our servant rather than our Lord. We expect Him to give us what we do not deserve, while we also expect Him to be satisfied with our most minimal offerings.

2. God is indeed so gracious to us that He gives us many things we have not asked for. If this were not the case, we would not find it so easy to demand more from Him. God's first and most fundamental mercies are absolute and free, but His subsequent and lesser mercies may be conditional. We find in scripture that all of God's promises concerning this life and eternal life are conditioned upon our obedience. The Jews, who had far greater promises of earthly blessings than Christians have, always had those promises upon the condition of their obedience. God expressly required

the performance of His commands for the Jews to receive His blessings, and made all of them forfeitable for failure to comply with His laws, as we see clearly laid out in the book of Deuteronomy. And under the gospel, Paul explains that God gives the "promises as well of this life, as of that to come unto godliness." 1 Timothy 4:8. Every man should therefore ask himself whether he has kept this condition or forfeited his claim by breaching the condition, even to the most ordinary blessings. For if he has so forfeited his claim then he has no basis to challenge God, but must rely entirely upon His unmerited favor.

3.   And here certainly "every mouth must be stopped, and all the world become guilty before God." Romans 3:19. For who among us can say that his obedience has matched his obligation? It is clear that we have all received abundantly from God's hand, but what has He received from ours? I ask the best of you to consider his best day, and ask if his receipts have not infinitely exceeded his disbursements: whether for any one good thing he has done, has he not received many more. And this disparity is not merely in number, but much more so in value. God's works are perfect. Like the first six days of creation, they "are all very good." Genesis 1. But on the contrary, our very "righteousness is as filthy rags," Isaiah 64:6. We offer to Him "the blind and the lame," Malachi 1:8, a few yawning, drowsy prayers, while the full current of our thoughts runs towards our secular and sinful concerns. We give only a few scanty alms, while our vanity competes with God. We may listen to a sermon for an hour, but it is more for the eloquence of the preacher than to seriously consider God's word. Like the duller sort of animals, we like to have our itching ears scratched, but we do not like to actually do what we are taught to do. All our service is maimed and imperfect if not actually corrupt. God may chastise us as He did Israel, "offer it now to the governor, will he be pleased with it?" Malachi 1:8. Our sinful treatment of our most holy things is enough to defeat any pretense we may

have to receive good things from the hand of God. Yet God knows that this is often the best of us, and many cannot even do that. For many, there can be no criticism concerning the blemishes of their sacrifices, for they offer none at all. Of them, we may say with the psalmist, "God is not in all their thoughts," Psalm 10:4. Many squander all of their time without remembering in whose "hand their time is." Psalm 31:15. Many enjoy the services of inferior creatures without considering that they are creatures who owe service to God. They live as if they were independent; as if they had created themselves, and owed no duty to God who is their true creator. How then can those who remove themselves from the family of God yet expect to receive the provisions which are intended for that family? Yet they have the impudence to complain if they do not receive what they need, or more likely merely what they lust for. They actually profane God's holy name in their impatience, as if He were merely their caterer or steward.

4. Let us seriously consider how remarkable is the patience of God; who notwithstanding the poor efforts of believers and the actual contempt of unbelievers, still routinely showers His bounty upon us. Justice would certainly not require Him to do so, for we have not fulfilled our part of the compact, and fail to even be grateful. We may say with David, "is this after the manner of men, O Lord?" 2 Samuel 7:19. No human indulgence could compare to this divine clemency. Our patience would be exhausted by one one-thousandth of our provocations.

5. We do not act as reasonable creatures should. For we have forfeited all of our rights, and yet keep all those great blessings only because of God's favor to us; and still we grow mutinous because some trifling thing is denied to us. One would think that such stupid ingratitude were not possible! If any one of us were a landlord and had a tenant who forfeited his lease by failing to pay his rent, it would be remarkable

enough if we did not evict that tenant. What would we think of him if he demanded that his cottage be adorned with a marble floor and a golden roof? Yet this is how we behave to our great Landlord. We grow angry if we do not have what we fancy and we ignore the important things which we have only because of His indulgence. Could anything be more unreasonable than this? Because of reason if not because of piety, let us then have a more genuine attitude. Rather than thinking so fondly of our appetites, let us reflect upon the fact that we hold what we do not by legal right but only by God's superabundant mercy. Let us have an appropriate fear of losing what we hold because of the shear insolence of our demands. When we think of what we want, let us remember how short we have come in our duty, and we will realize that we do not deserve the things which we desire. We will find cause to sit down and say with honest Mephibosheth, "What right have I to cry any more unto the King?" 2 Samuel 19:28. And if this be our conclusion based merely upon considering our imperfections and omissions, what must we conclude if we consider our actual sins? If the spots upon our sacrifices are provoking, how much more so our bold and profane disobedience? If those who neglect or forget God are listed among His enemies, what shall we say of those who actively defy Him? Indeed, if we look soberly upon the world and see how boldly people daily affront the Divine Majesty, we cannot but wonder why these perversions and profanities do not bring about the same ruin which came upon Sodom, or the earth open up and swallow us as happened to Korah. Numbers 16.

6.   God's long suffering mercy is shown not only to mankind in general, but to each of us in particular. And if each of us searches his conscience, he will find many reasons why God should bring severe discipline upon him, instead of the leniency and compassion which we find. And none of us suffers anything near what he could suffer. God exempts us far more than He afflicts us. But we accuse Him of that which

offends His sovereignty and honor. And we war against Him when we "yield our members instruments of unrighteousness." Romans 6:13. And we do this also with our souls and our minds, making excuses and taking on disguises. Our affections madly rush on "like the horse into the battle," Jeremiah 8:6, so that we sin in both attitude and action.

7.   How then can we be hostile to God and yet expect anything other than hostility from Him? And if He were to show us even the lowest degree of His anger, we would be lost. It is a good thing for us that God knows the impotence of our wild attempts and shows us pity for our follies. Were it not for this, we would not be in the position to continue to provoke Him, but instead would be defeated, and like Lot's wife, made into a monument of divine vengeance.

8.   How much then do we owe to the mercy and compassion of our God, that "He suffers not His whole displeasure to arise," Psalm 78:39, but instead holds back the just severity which He might use towards us? Anyone condemned to the gallows would consider it a great mercy to escape with a lesser penalty. Why then do we have such poor thoughts towards God when He corrects us so lightly, as if our thoughts and actions were not the affront to His honor which they in fact are? Let him who is the most innocent among us consider his sins and his sufferings, and he will find a vast inequality between them. And let him not think for a moment that his sins are not so bad just because he does not receive the punishment which he deserves. He sins often but is disciplined rarely, and then most lightly. God does this with regret and reluctance. "How shall I give thee up, O Ephraim?" Hosea 11:8. When these disparities are considered, we must certainly join heartily in Ezra's confession, "Thou O God has punished us less than our iniquities deserve." Ezra 9:13.

9.   We also tend to complain about these light disciplines which we may receive, which may itself cause God to turn our whips into scorpions, as He threatened Israel, "to punish us

yet seven times more" Leviticus 26:18. Yet even this does not quickly exasperate Him. The history of Israel shows how long He could bear a murmuring generation. Yet we as the new Israel, are at greater risk: "yet let us not be high-minded but fear." Romans 11:20. We see that though God delayed the doom which fell upon Israel, and preceded it with miraculous judgments, yet not one of those murmurers entered Canaan. And we also see that whereas God's denunciations of other sins were conditional and reversible, yet this was bound with an oath; "He swore in His wrath that they should not enter into His rest." Psalm 95:11. If we compare the hardships of the Israelites in the wilderness with most of our own sufferings, we must confess that there is less cause for us to grow mutinous and therefore much less excuse. From this, it is reasonable to infer that we face a greater danger if we persist. It shows us the greatness of God's long suffering towards us that He yet allows us space to reform. How foolish it is for us to make new complaints when we have not given account for our past ones. I fear that the most resigned one of us would find upon recollection that He has murmured even more than Israel did. Therefore we should fear that we may yet suffer plagues as they did and that these may be irrevocable.

10. For all of these reasons, we ought not to complain even about our heaviest pressures. Instead we should consider that for many of us, our sin justly causes our sufferings, because they are the consequence of our own actions. Solomon tells us that he who "loves pleasure shall be a poor man," and that a "whorish woman will bring a man to a piece of bread." Proverbs 6:26. He also says that 'he that sits long at the wine shall have redness of eyes," Proverbs 23:29-30, and "that the slothful soul shall suffer hunger." Proverbs 19:15. These things do not happen because of God's affliction, but because they are the natural consequences of these vices. God has so ordered things that sin naturally causes its own punishment. He is not required to take any special action.

We punish ourselves. Our own backslidings reprove us," Jeremiah 2:19, "and our iniquities are" of themselves enough to "become our ruin." Ezekiel 18:30.

11. Every man should therefore ask Himself if the troubles he labors under are of this sort. Is the poverty he complains of caused by his own wastefulness, sloth or negligence? When he cries out that "his comeliness is turned into corruption," Daniel 10:8, have his visits to the harlot's house made "rottenness enter into his bones?" Habakkuk 3:16. If he is beset with contentions, and has wounds without cause, has he "not tarried long at the wine?" If he has lost a friend, has he by some treacherous wound caused him to depart? If he lies under infamy, is it merely the echo of his own scandalous crimes? If he finds this to be true, surely his mouth should be closed. He cannot without impudence complain of anyone or anything but himself. He cannot claim ignorance that such effects would flow naturally from such causes. If he chooses the cause, he must accept the effect also. No man could be so insane as to think that God would miraculously disjoin what by nature He has joined just so that man may sin at ease and have any bestial pleasure he desires without any consequences. We read indeed that God divided the sea, but it was to make "a way for the ransomed of the Lord to pass over," Isaiah 51:10. He did this for His own people who followed His command, but when they were safely through, the waters immediately returned to their channel and overwhelmed the Egyptians, who went forth apart from God's command and protection. And surely this is also the case for us. No man may expect to avoid the natural consequences of his sin, and may only expect God's miraculous intervention when he is obeying the Lord.

12. As unreasonable as it is to accuse God for the ill effects of our own sin, it is even worse to complain because we possess insufficient materials to allow us to sin even more. I fear that this is the case with many of us, who are discontented

because others possess greater luxuries, and we covet more and more expensive and luxurious possessions. These are those of whom James speaks, "who ask amiss, that they may consume it upon their lusts." James 4:3. And this kind of mutiny is often acted out with frenzy. Would any sane man tell another that he intended to cut his throat, and then ask him to supply the knife? Yet this is what we are really doing when we murmur against God for not giving us the very things with which we intend to wage war against Him! For surely many of our discontents are just like this. Each of us then should examine himself, and if he does so honestly, he will find that for the small bits of obedience he offers to God, he receives an abundance of mercies, both spiritual and physical. God as much underpays him for his sins, as he overrates his own service to God. This shows that God does not delight in our affliction, and how gladly He takes any small occasion to caress and cherish us, rather than punish us. This consideration ought to cause us to grieve for our sin and to desire to please God. We should say with the prophet Daniel, "O Lord, to us belongs confusion of face, but to the Lord our God belong mercies and forgiveness, though we have rebelled against Him." Daniel 9:8-9. We should revere God when we are afflicted, and we should acknowledge His wisdom in His disposition of events in the lives of individuals, as are consistent with His economy and management of the world.

SECTION VI

Of God's General Providence

1. When God created the universe, He intended to glorify Himself in this one magnificent act of His unlimited power, and then to leave this demonstration for all to see, as the "ostrich her eggs" in the wilderness, Lamentations 4:3. And having drawn the universe out of the first chaos, He secured it from returning to chaos by establishing a symmetry of parts and a regular order of motion. Thus it is that the heavens have their constant revolutions, the earth its succession of seasons and the animals their course of generation and corruption. By this wise economy, the world after many ages seems still in its spring and its first beauty. But all of this would have been in vain if He had not also made man to enjoy it and to rest in His care. However, rather than using his reason to appreciate creation, man has used it to create confusion. Job compares him "to the wild ass's colt," Job 11:12, which wanders the world without acknowledging the common good. God has therefore hedged in this unruly creature by setting a fence of laws about him, both natural laws and laws given by special revelation. God has taken man into the common circle of His providence, so that he, as well as the rest of creation, has his particular station assigned to him, not only in reference to other creatures, but also in reference to other men. God has ordained ranks and classes among

men and endowed them with special and appropriate qualifications for those stations where He has put them.

2. This is a work of the infinite wisdom of God; and it is of unspeakable advantage to men. Without this regular disposure, the world would have been in the same confusion which we read of in the host of the Midianites, "every man's sword against his fellow," Judges 7:22. Nothing but force could determine who should possess anything or have the right to do anything. And even that decision would be repealed when a greater force appeared. So we have every reason to acknowledge the value of the order which God has established among men. Even he who is assigned the lowest place in this order is infinitely happier by contributing to that general harmony than he could ever be in any state of discord.

3. If this were well considered, I think that it would silence all of our complaints, and we would not be so extremely concerned about in what part of the structure it pleases the architect to put us. Every man should consider himself to be but a small portion of the material with which the greater form is constructed. Not every stone is fit to be the cornerstone. Not every rafter is fit to be the main beam. It is for the wisdom of the Master Builder to determine where each part belongs. And to argue with God about where we are placed is to show direct contempt for His wisdom. If God has sufficient wisdom to construct this vast and beautiful fabric, how can we question where each thread is placed? Did He by His "wisdom make the heavens, and by His understanding stretch out the clouds?" Proverbs 3:19. Shall He not know where to put each little lump of clay upon the earth? It is utterly absurd to question this, and yet that is exactly what we do when we complain about the condition He has placed us in.

4. The truth is that we are all so full of ourselves that we find it hard to see anything beyond ourselves. Every one of us

expects that God should place him where he has a mind to be, and does not think about where he fits into God's total plan. But God considers the whole of mankind, and His plan is not subject to the desires of any one person. "He has made the great and the small, and cares for all alike." Wisdom 6:7. He is the common Father of Mankind and disposes all things for the good of this great family. He will not withdraw from His design and method in order to satisfy the impatient cravings of one demanding child. We would not be pleased with an earthly king who indulged one favorite person to the disadvantage of the public. Yet we murmur at God for failing to do this very thing.

5. Each of us should consider that others have the same desires that we have. If we do not like to live in humble circumstances, we should remember that others feel the same way. "Whose voice shall the Lord hear?" Ecclesiasticus 34:24. How insolent it is for me to think that God should humor me more than anyone else. The more impatient I am, the less likely am I to get what I desire, for such an attitude does not render me a darling to God. And God cannot satisfy everyone equally for we all desire to be superior to others. We all desire not only to keep our current wealth, but to attain more. How could that happen if others did not lose the wealth which they now have? It could only happen if God made a miraculous multiplication of treasure for mankind's desire alone as the Lord multiplied the loaves to satisfy their hunger. Matthew 16:9. It was a good answer which the ambassadors of an oppressed province made to Anthony, "if O Emperor, you will have double taxes from us, you must help us to double springs and harvests." God would have to double His creation if He were to satisfy all the unreasonable appetites of men. And if God does not do this for everyone, why should any one of us expect Him to do it for him?

6. As unreasonable as this is, most of us show by our thoughts and actions that this is how we actually think. No one seems

to be upset about the fact that some are rich and that others are poor, and that some have risen higher in the world than others. But if it is he himself who is poor and of low esteem he will cry out that it is unjust. This attitude is an indication that he really thinks that the God who governs others should serve him, and give to him not what God thinks best, but what he himself thinks best. It is this self-love which is the spring and root of most of our complaints. It makes us fundamentally unfair and unqualified to make judgments about our own circumstances. It prompts us to make all kinds of exceptions for ourselves, as David did for his sons, "See that thou hurt not the young man Absolom." 2 Samuel 18:5. We expect God to manage the world with a particular regard to our liking.

7. Indeed, any thoughtful person should be astonished to consider that although God has disposed all things by His unerring wisdom, yet hardly anyone is pleased. The truth is that we are very content to see multitudes beneath us, but impatient to see any above us. To use the Apostle's illustration, "the foot complains that it is not the hand, and the ear because it is not the eye." I Corinthians 12:15-16. Not only the lower classes of men, but even the highest, complain if there are any above them. So foolish is this attitude that men feel compelled to feed it, if only with air and shadows. He who cannot raise himself in reality will do it by putting on airs. And when this becomes obvious to others, he will find that he has fallen in their estimation. The world seems to be so over run with this vanity that it is difficult to draw distinctions with respect to the extent of it. We cannot judge a person's true status by observing how he acts or what he seems to possess.

8. It appears then that men look upon themselves only as single persons, without reference to the community of which they are members. For if they did consider that, they would accept the places where they have been set and endeavor to

fulfill the duties of their positions, rather than continuously seeking to change them. A tree that is every year transplanted will never bear fruit. And a mind that is always hurried from its proper station will never do good in any station. As Solomon put it, "as a bird that wanders from its nest, so is a man that wanders from his place." Proverbs 27:8. It is easy to see what will happen to young ones from whom the mother wanders or to see what will happen to an estate whose owner is always off searching for another. We have many examples of this both in the church and in the government. We forget that we are all servants of the same master, and that it is up to Him in what office we shall serve Him. How would we like it if we had a servant who left his work undone because he wanted a higher office? Yet we repeat this insolence every day towards God. We sullenly dispute His orders and unless we may choose our own employment, we will do nothing.

9. It is evident that this perverse attitude of people breeds a great deal of mischief and disturbance in the world. And it would cause unlimited confusion and destruction if God permitted it to go unchecked. And if He allows even one ambitious person to break loose at any time, what great destruction happens as part of His judgment against us all. As is said of Nebuchadnezzar, he will "cause the whole earth to tremble, and shake kingdoms." Isaiah 14:16. And this may be said of many other robbers which have arisen. But if every person who aspired to wealth and power were to go unleashed, where would be sufficient fuel to maintain that great fire? No doubt every age produces men with such unbounded desires as Alexander or Caesar, but God does not allow them the same opportunities to trouble the world. And this is also true for the more petty ambitions of ordinary men who cannot find sufficient wind to fill their sails. He that set bounds to the sea, saying "hitherto shalt thou come and no farther, and though the waves thereof toss themselves, yet they cannot prevail, though they roar, yet

can they not pass over," Jeremiah 5:22, He does also depress the swelling pride of men, hanging weights upon them to hold them down. Although we are quite willing to forget it, yet God remains the Lord of the universe and He will assert his dominion over it. The most daring and clever plan which man can invent cannot prevail against God's authority. "The Lord will still be King, be the people ever so impatient." Psalm 99:1. It is therefore prudent, as well as our duty, to "be still, and know that He is God." Psalm 46:10. We should humble our own wills and submit to His. We should not provoke Him whom we cannot subdue. We may, like anxious horses, paw and fret, but God still holds the reins and keeps the bridle in our jaws, and we cannot advance a single step unless He permits it. Why then should we torment ourselves by our complaints, which only drive us further away from our true goal? God has revealed that it is His method to exalt the lowly. This is seen in the first two kings of Israel, who were chosen by God out of humble circumstances; one searching for his father's donkeys and the other keeping his father's sheep. If men would honestly and diligently apply themselves to the business of their proper calling they might find it to be a more direct path to advancement than all the sinister acts which the ambition of men causes them to pursue. Solomon sets this down as a basic principle. "Seest thou a man diligent in his business? He shall stand before kings. He shall not stand before mean men." Proverbs 22:29. But whether it has that effect or not, it will still sweeten his present condition, for it will divert his mind from mutinous reflections upon the higher positions of other men and upon his own lowly position. For it is precisely those men who do not mind their work who find the leisure time to gaze elsewhere. He that applies himself to his own business will find his thoughts more concentrated, which itself produces happiness. For it is looking too much abroad, and looking on the conditions of others, which causes an uproar at home. The son of Syrach speaks glowingly of the condition of he who labors and is content, and calls it "a sweet life." Ecclesiasticus 40:18. And certainly it is more so than the life of the greatest prince whose mind swells beyond his territories.

10. Upon consideration of all of this, clearly the reasonable thing to do is to leave God to govern the world, and not, like the sons of Zebedee, to seek the highest positions. We must learn to rest continually where He has placed us and allow Him to advance us and not our own designs. There is nowhere to hide from His eyes. As He valued the widow's mite above the great gifts of the rich, so He will accept the humble endeavors of the ordinary above the services of the powerful. For He has declared that He accepts "according to what a man has, and not according to what he does not have." 2 Corinthians 8:12. So wherever a man finds that he has been set, there he has the opportunity to approve himself to God. And though in the eyes of the world he may be a vessel of dishonor, yet in the day when God comes to "make up His jewels," Malachi 3:17, there will be another estimate made of those who have worked within their own spheres. Surely he that accepts this is happier than he that enjoys worldly splendor, and far happier than he who desires riches but cannot attain them. For such a man continuously tortures himself and cannot be satisfied. Let therefore our comfort as well as our duty prompt us to accept and submit to God's distribution of all things, for God shows His distinct care for each individual by giving to him what really is best for him.

SECTION VII

Of God's Particular Providence

1.   It is characteristic of our finite nature that we cannot attend to multiple things at once, and that the more we focus on one thing, the greater will be our neglect of other things. But God does not have this limitation. His eyes see everything simultaneously. He attends to all of the most distant and different things at the same time. And He does not withdraw Himself from the concerns of men for His own benefit. Though He has His "dwelling so high, yet He humbles Himself to behold the things in heaven and earth." Psalm 113:5-6. Nor does He confine Himself to the greater and more magnificent things, but His attention descends to the lowest parts of His creation; to the birds of the air and to the lilies of the field. And surely our Savior's statement is undebatable, "are ye not much better than they?" Matthew 6:26. As He told His disciples, if a sparrow cannot fall to the ground without His particular notice, then surely no human being is considered any less by Him than they are. And if the very hairs of our heads are all numbered, then we cannot think that such hairs are more important than the whole person. We must conclude that God does indeed focus His attention upon all of the particular concerns of every person.

2. Since God is infinitely good, this attention which He gives to each one of us cannot have any harmful purpose. He watches over us as a guardian, not as a spy. He looks to help us to accept His blessings. His grace is designed to be for our advantage and His wisdom is the basis for how He dispenses it to us. "All things," says the "wise man, are not profitable for all men." Ecclesiasticus 37:28. Indeed nothing is absolutely good but God Himself. All created things are either good or bad only in reference to that to which they are applied. Food is good, but to an overfed stomach it is actually dangerous. Fire is good, but if we try to hold it, it will burn both our clothing and our flesh. And as human wisdom teaches us how to properly use these things, so divine wisdom orders events according to what is best for the person concerned. "He knows our frame," Psalm 103:14, and discerns what effect anything will have upon us. We do not really know ourselves and do not know what effect things or events will have upon us. We make merely random guesses and poor choices. If we acknowledge God's providence, goodness and wisdom, as all Christians should, this acknowledgement will be our defense against our own anxiety, demands and complaints. We cannot think that our suffering is not noticed by Him who sees all. And we cannot think that our difficulties are designed to harm us, because all things ultimately come from Him who intends only good for us. Nor can we think that God's good intentions could go wrong, for they are guided by infinite and unerring wisdom and backed by unlimited power. Surely this consideration should be to us, as the Apostle says, "strong consolation," Hebrews 6:18, if we would but duly apply it.

3. Because general principles tend to make only a slight impression upon us, it may be useful to consider the application of those principles to the different types of our discontents. Basically these discontents fall into two categories: Either we are troubled because we do not have something

which we desire, or we are suffering something which we want to avoid.

4.   The first of these is usually the most comprehensive, for most of us are more tormented because of something we want than because of any pain which we feel. Indeed, our desires are so exorbitant that they provide much room for discontent. But it is certain that our desires do not produce any charm which outweighs the consideration that God is wise and discerning and is careful to provide what is really good for us. We are poor blind creatures, and we look only on the surface of things. If we see some beautiful thing which stirs up our senses, we pursue it earnestly. But God penetrates deeper. He sees to the very bottom of who we are and He sees the true value of what we desire. He knows that things which may please our appetites may actually harm our health. He will not more give them to us than a father would give his child the golden poison he cries for. Perhaps a man is taken with the enchanting music of fame and does not like his own obscure position. He desires to present himself upon a public theater to draw the attention of the world. But he does not know how well he shall perform there, and whether he shall draw applause or hisses. He may merely make himself a public spectacle of scorn. Or if he does not, he may fill up his vain glory to such a bulk as renders him too great a weight for that tottering pinnacle upon which he stands, and he may fall back to his original obscure position. Another may no less eagerly desire wealth and think that if he possesses treasures that he will be happy. But he does not know what he will do with it. There are two contrary temptations that come with riches. They may lead either to riotous living or to covetousness for still more. He is foolish who convinces himself that he can avoid these temptations. Also, the more money a man has, the more he is subject to those who would seek to take it from him. Many a man may not have died so poor if he had not lived so rich. Another perhaps wants children to leave what he does have to, and

complains with Abraham, "Lord what wilt Thou give me, seeing I go childless?" Genesis 15:2. Yet how does he know whether that child he so much desires "shall be a wise man or a fool?" Ecclesiastes 2:19. Will it be a comfort or a vexation to live to find out? Rachel sought this satisfaction with the greatest impatience; "give me children, or I die." Genesis 30:1. And it is plainly seen that receiving her desire proved to be the loss of her life.

5. In these and in many other instances, we push forward blindfolded, and very often impetuously pursue that which would ruin us. If God did not prevent it, what precipices would we rush towards? If He responded to our demands more than to our true needs, we would quickly sink under the weight of our own desires, and perish as a result of obtaining what we seek. Any man that soberly reflects upon the events of his life must admit that he has sometimes desired things which would have done him great harm if he had obtained them, and would now look upon the denial of those things as a great mercy. On the other side, when he has succeeded in obtaining what he sought after, it has been like the quails to the Israelites, a conviction and punishment rather than satisfaction. And now surely God may complain about us as He did about Israel, "How long will it be ere you believe me?" Numbers 14:11. After all the proof He has given us of His care for us, and after all the folly we have shown by insisting on making our own decisions, we still cannot be brought to the point of distrusting ourselves and placing our full reliance upon Him! We still want to make our own choices and see God as merely the way to get what we want.

6. This is a strange perverseness, and no sensible man would be guilty of it in any other instance. In all our secular affairs we trust those whom we have cause to think understand them better than ourselves. We put our estates into the lawyer's hand and our bodies into the physician's. We submit

to their advice even when it is against our mood merely because we consider them to be better judges than ourselves. Yet we cannot be persuaded to give this same deference to God. We still attempt to tell Him what to do and become very angry if what He gives us does not exactly match our fancy. Can we offend God in any other way greater than to distrust Him? It is to deny either His wisdom or His goodness or both, and so to derogate Him with respect to two of His essential attributes. For there can be no rational reason given by anyone who believes that God has those attributes for not trusting all of their concerns to Him. For surely in all of human discourse there is no more indisputable principle than that for our own sakes we ought to resign ourselves to Him who can and will make better choices for us than we are capable of making ourselves.

7. This principle was so obvious by mere natural reason, that Socrates advised men to pray only for blessings in general and to leave the particular types of blessings to God to decide, because He alone knows what is the most good for us. And this advice from a heathen should embarrass us Christians who have failed to see it. It is surely an offense to God that we who profess to know Him more should trust Him less. So we see that our complaints do not end with their own guilt, but actually rise to a form of blasphemy. By our complaints and our impatience we accuse God of failing in His wisdom, power and love to meet our true needs. By doing this, we act like practical atheists.

8. And this consideration also addresses the other type of our discontents; those which arise out of our suffering. For our actual afflictions, as well as the things which cause them, may be for us less bitter if we but consider that it is the very same goodness and wisdom which denies us things which are harmful to us which also gives us distasteful things which may actually be profitable for us. It is not always enough to limit what we take in. Sometimes things must be

taken away from us. And surely nothing both cleanses and purifies the soul more than afflictions, if we do not frustrate their true purpose by the way we react to them.

61

SECTION VIII

Of the Advantage of Afflictions

1.   It would take an entire volume to give a complete account of the benefits of afflictions. I will point out only some of the more general and obvious benefits. The first is that they awaken us to God's call to repentance. And this is the most common purpose. Consider what God said in Hosea 5:15; "I will go and return to my place, till they acknowledge their offense, and seek my face: in their affliction, they will seek me early." In the very next verse we see the response of the people; "Come and let us return unto the Lord: for He hath torn and He will heal us; He hath smitten and He will bind us up." We see this same thing in the brothers of Joseph. Although there was a long time between their ill treatment of him and his pretense of harshness to them, yet Joseph's actions caused them to remember what they had done, saying, "we are verily guilty concerning our brother." Genesis 42:21. Prosperity is an intoxicating thing, and there are few minds strong enough to bear it. It puts us to sleep and amuses us with pleasant dreams, while all the time Satan rifles through our treasures, and by the deceitful charms of sin, he robs us of our innocence and our true happiness. Can there be anything more valuable for a true friend to do than to rouse such a man from his sleep and to help him to see the evil designs which are laid against him? This is an

important purpose of afflictions. We should look on them as our friends and companions for they are intended to rescue us, and to warn us of the real enemies which silently attack us. He that complains of these afflictions and sees them as his "enemies because they tell him the truth," Galatians 4:16, does miserably pervert "the counsel of God against himself." Luke 7:30. He chooses to see them as the wounds of an enemy rather than what they really are, the corrections of a Father.

2. While afflictions serve to admonish us of sins in a very general way, it frequently pleases God to make the affliction match the sin, so that the very image of the sin is seen in the affliction. It is the dark shadow that attends the happy delight of the moment. The author of The Wisdom of Solomon observes that the turning of the Egyptian waters into blood was a manifest reproof of that cruel command to murder the Hebrew infants. Wisdom 12:5. In most, if not all of our sufferings, we may see some such corresponding circumstances which show that they are effects which naturally follow a cause. God does all things in specific number, weight and measure. And in punishments also, we may observe a symmetry and proportion. God adapts them not only to the severity but also to the specific kind of sin. The only fixed rule which was given to human authorities for punishment of crimes was in the case of murder, which we see to be grounded in this rule of proportion: "he that sheddeth man's blood, by man shall his blood be shed." Genesis 9:6. And while God has recinded for us the rule of an "eye for the eye, the tooth for the tooth," Exodus 21:24 (probably because our vengeful natures and hard hearts were too pleased with it), yet He has not indicated that He Himself would not act in accordance with it. We see that He often causes men to feel the pain of the very injustice which they directed towards others. Scripture gives us many examples of this, such as Adonibezek in Judges 1:6 and Ahab in I Kings 21:19. This method with which God proportions the punishment to the

sin may not always be evident on its face to the world. Yet I believe that if men would but reflect upon their own experiences, they would see that their calamities merely traced the footsteps of their sins.

3.   If we give this its proper consideration, we must admit that it is for our benefit. We have a natural blindness when we look within ourselves. We need to be given a proper light to allow us to see correctly what is in us. Since the purpose of our afflictions is our repentance, it is good for us that God designs them to show up those particular sins for which He wants us to repent. The whole body of our sin will not be destroyed all at once, but must be dismembered limb by limb. He that tries to remove it at once will fail, but he who does it piece by piece may quickly succeed. It is a great part of spiritual wisdom to know where the strength of our corruptions lies. And it is a great example of God's care for us that by His corrections and discipline He instructs us where and how to deal with them.

4.   Therefore, it should be our intent to critically observe our afflictions; not to increase our complaints, but to learn from them where our weaknesses lie. This is "to hear the rod, and who hath appointed it." Micah 6:9. Let him that suffers in any of his concerns ask himself whether there is in him a corresponding guilt which explains it, "as face answers face." Proverbs 27:19. Let he who suffers loss in his possessions consider how they were acquired, whether there was any fraud or injustice involved. And if he does not find that, then let him consider how he has used his wealth, whether to satisfy his own desires or just to take pride in looking upon it. Of if he suffers illness, let him ask whether it was the result of his own actions, or whether he has used his strength and health for purposes other than those for which it was given, and for this reason it was taken from him. Let he who suffers shame ask whether or not it is deserved, in whole or in part, or if not, then let him consider whether

some secret and concealed sin would have brought such shame if it were known. If so, then the loss of reputation is just, and God may take it away by either a just or an unjust accusation. And if his heart does not accuse him of this, yet let him consider whether his own pride or vanity has made this a necessary and appropriate humiliation for him. Or let him remember how he has behaved towards others. In these and many other instances, such an inward examination would likely show the connection between our guilt and our afflictions, and by showing the spring from which they flow, also show how to stop the current. He who makes this examination would find less cause for complaints and more direction for his own reformation. He would "accept of the punishment of his iniquity, and thank the Lord for thus giving him warning." Psalm 16:8.

5. A second benefit which God gives to us through our afflictions is to wean us from the world; to disentangle us from its charms and its chains, and thus to draw us to Himself. We read in the story of the flood that so long as the earth was covered with water, the raven was content to take shelter in the ark, but when the earth was fair and dry, the dove abandoned it. Genesis 8:12. And so it is with us. Even the worst of men will cry out to God in a time of great distress. Remember that the heathen mariners rebuked Jonah for not calling upon his God. Jonah 1:6. And the very best of us are likely to forget God in times of ease and prosperity. The world may often enchant us and capture us. And so it is a sign of God's care for us that He sometimes allows us to see the more ugly side of the world, that we may run for shelter into the arms of our Father. If everything here on earth satisfied our moods and desires, when would we think to return to Him? And if we never saw the signs of death, how could we be prepared for it? The story is told that Antigonus, a general serving under Alexander the Great, saw a soldier in his camp who was both daring and courageous, often exposing himself to great risk. But he also suffered a

great illness. When he was healed from that illness, he grew more cautious and would no longer expose himself to risk. When asked why this was the case, the soldier replied that now that he was healthy, his life was of value to him, and he would no longer risk it as he did when his life was a burden to him. I fear that many of us would be like that soldier if God were to cure us of all maladies and put us at ease. We would think our lives too precious to be surrendered to Him, much less to be risked for His sake, as our faith teaches us it should be. The Son of Syrach observes how "dreadful death is to a man that is at rest in his possessions, that hath abundance of all things, and hath nothing to vex him." Eccleseasticus 41:1. The truth is that we so passionately dote upon the world, that like enchanted lovers, we can bear much ill treatment before we will abandon our pursuit. Any little favor from the world will so charm us that we must be disciplined by repeated disappointments before we will withdraw our confidence from it. How fatally secure would we feel if God were to permit this siren always to entertain us with her sweet music, and never to allow discordant and grating notes to interrupt our raptures and to awaken us to sober thinking?

6.   Indeed, it is one of the greatest demonstrations of God's love for us, and also of His mercy, that He protects us from being reduced to the condition of being caught in the spell of the world. Our very connection to God through our baptism included a denunciation of the world, and is much like a marriage to Him, so that we cannot without disloyalty to Him again throw ourselves into its embraces. To do so is to break our "covenant with God." Proverbs 2:17. He does not pursue us with a jealous rage, nor with the severity which our breach of the covenant would justify, and He does not divorce us. Instead He seeks to reclaim us and to bring us back to Himself. The extent of this leniency is well stated by the prophet with respect to Israel: "They say, if a man may put away his wife, and she become another man's, shall he

return to her again? But thou hast played the harlot with many lovers, yet return unto me saith the Lord." Jeremiah 3:1. And this remarkable illustration does not overstate the extent of the mercy which He shows us every day. Even though we have in effect committed adultery with the world, and taken the affections to which God has a right, and given them to the world instead, yet He does not abandon us to the natural consequences of such action. Instead He invites us to return to Him. And since the mere invitation is often insufficient to get us to actually turn, He actively seeks to break our connection to the world. He does this by removing the disguise in which the world courted us and causing us to see it for what it is, a scene of "vanity and vexation of spirit." Ecclesiastes 1:14.

7. And as God does this in general, so He also does it in regard to those specific worldly satisfactions which most strongly claim our affections. We are not so much endangered by those things to which we are indifferent. It is those things upon which we have set our hearts which become a snare to us and which awaken the jealousy of God. It is therefore in those things that He challenges us. We often see that those who are enamored by their own beauty suffer some disease or accident which diminishes it and makes their winter overtake their spring. And we also see that we often loose friendships which have become inordinately important to us. If one of our children is too fondly favored over the others, it is likely that harm will come to that child, and our joy and love will be turned into grief and sorrow. When God sees our hearts so excessively cleave to any transitory thing, He knows that it is necessary to sever it from us; for while we hold to such things, which interfere with our relationship to God, "our souls cleave to the dust," Psalm 119:25, and we cannot soar up to the higher region for which our souls were designed.

8. All of this is to say that God loves us so much that He will remove any obstruction to our intimate union with Him. He deeply desires this relationship. So while He may not directly compensate us for any loss we may experience, how could we possibly be angry when He has shown such love and kindness to us? And consider also that He takes away from us empty illusions and false contentment so that He may instead give us freely durable and lasting joys. We show how very ignorant we are as to what is in our own best interests, not to mention our insensitivity to our obligations to God, when we complain and fail to acknowledge that He holds us in His caring hands. It is true indeed that we have adhered so closely to things which should never have been attached to us, that they cannot be removed without some pain. For the sake of our own earthly security, we can and must endure the removal of things which have become a part of us by growing into us over time. He who has a leg which is full of gangrene will allow the surgeon to remove it and will thank him for doing so. But where our souls are concerned, and where the part which needs to be removed in order to save us is not a natural created part, but merely affixed to us by our own passions, we resist God's surgery and complain that we would rather die than loose the part which we love so much. In summary, although God is exceedingly patient and long suffering, yet He will not stoop so low as to share what is rightfully His with the world, if we have become devoted to it. Our empty forms of service will not satisfy Him. If He cannot divorce our hearts from the world, He will divorce Himself from us. This being the case, we are foolish if we do not willingly submit to His method with us and happily allow whatever surgery is required, no matter how sharp the knife may be. We can make the process quicker and easier by cooperating, or we can make it more difficult and painful by struggling against it. Let us therefore surrender our wills to Him and allow Him to remove any offending part from us, and by doing so, make the process

easier. And if we have found it to be difficult and painful to be disentangled from the world, let us be all the more cautious about any future entanglements with it. If our escape has been, as the Apostle says, "so as by fire," Jude 23, with pain and injury, then let us at least have the wits which the common proverb allows to children and not again expose ourselves to the fire. Let us never again give our hearts to any external thing. We should let all of the concerns of the world hang loose about us. Then we shall not suffer injury whenever God calls for them. Or perhaps, He will not call for them at all, because we have not allowed them to draw our hearts from Him.

9. A third advantage of affliction is that it is a mark and signature of our adoption. It proves that we are legitimate children of God. The Apostle says, "what son is he whom the Father chastiseth not? But if he be without chastisement, whereof all are partakers, then are ye bastards and not sons." Hebrews 12:7-8. Jacob clothed his darling Joseph in a coat of many colors, and so also, God's chosen ones wear coats interwoven with a mixture of dark and gloomy colors. Their long white robes are laid up for them to wear at the marriage of the lamb. Revelation 19:7. Indeed, we greatly misunderstand the design and intent of our faith if we think that it calls us to a condition of ease and security. It is said of those who worshipped the golden calf that their intent was to "sit down to eat and to drink, and rise up to play." Exodus 32:6. But the disciples of the crucified Savior are trained to another discipline. We are entered into a state of warfare. We are not only servants of Christ's family but also soldiers of His camp. In a time of war, men must not expect to pass their time in ease and softness, but in addition to all of the dangers and difficulties of combat, they have other hardships to endure. They face hunger and thirst, heat and cold, hard lodgings and weary marches. He that cannot endure these things will not long remain loyal to his Commander's cause. And it is the same in our spiritual warfare. We face

much pressure and suffering, both when we are passive and when we are active. This is why our Savior admonishes us to count the costs of following Him. He does not seek to win us by easy terms, but warns us to expect the worst. He says that he "that forsakes not all that he hath shall not be My disciple," Luke 14:33, and "that through much tribulation enter into the Kingdom of God." Acts 14:22. Indeed, it would be absurd for us to expect easy conditions when we consider the hardships to which our Leader has submitted. "The Captain of our salvation was perfected by sufferings," Hebrews 2:10, "and if it behoved Christ to suffer" before He entered into His glory, Luke 24:46, then it is insolent madness for us to expect to be carried upon beds of ivory and to be entertained by the music of angels.

10.   Godly men have considered all this and come to look upon their secular prosperity with fear, and sought to take some cross upon their shoulders, thinking it a necessary sign of their sonship and their closeness to Christ. Why then should we seek to avoid the very burdens which they sought, and despise what they so valued? If we at all appreciate what a privilege it is to be the sons of God and fellow heirs with Christ, why do we complain about bearing any share of His suffering? The Roman captain told St. Paul that he paid a great sum of money to gain his Roman citizenship. Acts 22:28. Should we expect so much more noble and advantageous an adoption at no cost? Do we expect God to change His entire economy for our personal ease, and to give us our eternal inheritance without first allowing us any earthly burdens? This would be both and unjust and a vain hope. When David was given the opportunity of becoming the king's son-in-law, I Samuel 18:21, he put such a value upon the dignity of it that he did not mind the difficulties which came with it. We are very poor souls indeed if when an infinitely higher position is offered to us we are anxious about the hardships which come with it. Remember that the Apostle said "if we suffer, we shall also reign with Him." 2

Timothy 2:12. Although our afflictions are not joyous, but are grievous, yet when we consider that they are but a down payment on our future inheritance, they appear all together different, and enamor us rather than frighten us.

11.   A fourth advantage of afflictions is that they create and increase within us compassion towards others. There is nothing which so qualifies us to rightly estimate the suffering of others as to have ourselves felt them. Without this experience, our appreciation of the suffering of others is dull and confused, as is a blind man's concept of color or a deaf man's concept of music. They "that stretch themselves upon their couches, that eat the lambs out of the flock, and the calves out of the midst of the stall, that chant to the sound of the violin, drink wine in bowls, and anoint themselves with the chief ointments, will not much be grieved with the afflictions of Joseph." Amos 6:4-5. So necessary is our experience in order for us to feel the suffering of others, that we are told it was a requirement of our High Priest (that highest example of boundless compassion). Therefore the apostle said, "it behoved Him in all things to be made like His brethren; that He might be a merciful and faithful High Priest in things pertaining to God, to make reconciliation for the sins of the people: for in that He Himself hath suffered being tempted, He is able also to succor them that are tempted." Hebrews 2:17-18. If He whose very appreciation of our miseries caused Him to come down to us yet chose human form to advance His compassion for us, how necessary is suffering to open our insensitive hearts? And God has said that the measure of our mercy to our fellow man shall be the standard by which He apportions His mercy to us. It is then greatly to our advantage that we show greater mercy to others. For when He causes us to taste the bitter cup of the sufferings of others, He so grants to us a genuine sympathy for them, and by doing so qualifies us to receive a greater portion of His mercy. And there is not only profit but also honor in this. Compassion is one of the greatest

properties which human beings are capable of, and we demean ourselves when we put it off. And more than this, it is an attribute of God. The more we advance in it, the closer we may draw to Him. Therefore we have every reason to thank and bless Him for that discipline which promotes in us the excellent grace of compassion.

12.   A fifth benefit of affliction is that it improves our devotional life with the Lord. It makes our prayer life more earnest. While blessings and prosperity flow upon us, we bathe in their streams, but we forget their source. God will then stop the current and leave us dry so that our need will do what our gratitude would not, and cause us to seek the spring of all blessing and the author of all that is good. This effect of afflictions is observed by the prophet, "Lord, in trouble have they visited Thee, they poured out a prayer when Thy chastening was upon them." Isaiah 26:16. I believe that it is every man's experience that his prayers are more frequent and heartfelt when he is under some distress. It is then that we petition God, saying with Israel, "deliver us only we pray Thee this day: and they put away the strange gods from among them and served the Lord." Judges 10:15-16. It is a sad reflection upon us that we need to be so pressed before we will return to Him. It demonstrates God's mercy that when His exhortations will not get our attention, He will do what He must to claim us. And it is not His intention that our devotion should cease when a calamity ends, but that through it we may develop the habit of devotion. And indeed, we are worse than brutes if we do not react as He intends. We think it is rude to contact a man only when we want something from him, and to ignore him thereafter. Yet this is how we treat God. Should not God's mercy to us cause us to desire to seek Him daily? And if this consideration does not do so, should we not at least acknowledge that we will soon need His mercy again? God complains of Israel, "wherefore say my people, we are lords? We will come no more unto Thee." Jeremiah 2:31. It is an insolent folly to renounce our

dependence upon God whenever we no longer feel the pressure of our need. For our needs will likely soon spring up again. Do we then return to Him whom we ignored in the interim? If we have any good sense at all, we will thank Him for His past mercies and not just come begging whenever we are in need. We should acknowledge the benefit of those first calamities which inspired our devotion and taught us to pray in earnest. Let our thanks not be uttered in a fainter voice than our petitions! Let our daily concerns be brought to Him with the same fervency as when calamity strikes.

13. Not only is our devotional life improved through our afflictions, but so also are the graces of Godly character: our faith, hope, patience, ability to bear suffering, strength and courage. It is no triumph of faith to merely trust God for those good things which he so readily gives to us. That is to walk by feelings, not by faith. Real faith triumphs through adversity and destitution. "And against hope to believe in hope;" this is the faith of a true child of Abraham, and it will be imputed to us, as it was to him, "for righteousness." Romans 4:23. Also, we would have no opportunity to grow and exercise the essential character quality of patience if we never suffered afflictions. Patience is not a natural human trait, and cannot begin to be formed without adversity. Nor would there be any opportunity to exercise it. In times of prosperity, we may still employ temperance, humility and caution, but patience seems a useless virtue in such times, and may be counterfeit until it is tested by adversity. Yet it is patience that is the most glorious accomplishment of a Christian. It is that which most highly conforms him to the image of his Savior, whose entire earthly life was a perpetual exercise of this grace of patience. We love our ease entirely too much if we are unwilling to buy this pearl, though it be at great price.

14. Lastly, our thankfulness is actually increased by our distresses. While it is natural for us to think about those blessings

which we have lost, and doing so causes us great discontent, surely it is more rational for us to use that remembrance to inspire us to thankfulness for the times when those blessings were enjoyed. And not only our past enjoyments but also our present deprivations deserve our gratitude, if we properly consider the true advantages which we derive from them. If we bitterly refuse to acknowledge God's guiding hand in our experiences, we gain nothing from them, for we still stand answerable before Him for the good which He intended for us through them. We stand liable for a new charge of ingratitude for "despising the chastisement of the Lord." Hebrews 12:5.

15. If we fairly consider these benefits of afflictions, as incompletely as I have tried to describe them, we should be ready to acknowledge and accept even the sharpest of God's methods. If we do not, then we make ourselves to be merely like the animals who know only what their bodily senses convey to them. But if we have the ability to reason and to understand, and if we consider that we have immortal souls, then we must conclude that the interests of our souls far outweigh any suffering of the flesh. And if we consider merely our best interests here in this earthly life, we do still misjudge God's methods and complain when a little temporary uneasiness may be the path to greater happiness. When Moses fled out of Egypt, he did not know that he would return there and be like a "god to Pharoah." Exodus 4:16. And when Joseph was delivered there as a slave, he did not know that he would become a ruler there. As far apart as those conditions were, it was the providence of God to connect them and the later blessing could not have occurred without the prior distress. We may observe the same guiding hand at work in our own troubles, and that events in our lives which we have experienced with the greatest regret have turned out to be very beneficial to us.

16.   In conclusion, we have all the evidence and reason which is required to calm ourselves in our anxieties, to strengthen our faith and to cause us to trust God completely. For although we cannot fully understand His plans and intentions, yet we know that we have nothing to fear, unless it is caused by our own distrust and foolish actions. We have our Savior's promise to rely upon, that "He will not give us a stone when we ask for bread, nor a scorpion when we ask for a fish." Matthew 7:9. And His love secures us from the errors of our own wild choices, for He does not give us stones and scorpions when we seek after them. Let us then entrust our concerns to Him who knows them far better than we do ourselves, and make it our sole concern to accept His provisions with as much submission and duty as He has given them with love and wisdom. For if we can but do that, then all the powers of earth and hell cannot make us miserable. For whatever our afflictions may be, we can be sure that they are what we in some respect need to go through. Whether they are a form of deprivation or an event which comes upon us, we know that they are given by Him who cannot err and that we shall in the end have cause to say with the psalmist, "it is good for me that I have been afflicted." Psalm 119:71.

SECTION IX

Of our Misfortunes Compared with other Men's

1. Let us now consider that which is equally important; the comparing of our misfortunes with those which other men suffer and bear. If we will do that, we will soon see that we have little cause to think ourselves unusual or that our troubles are greater than those of others. There is no man living who can fairly consider himself to be the most unhappy man; for there are innumerable distresses suffered by others which he knows nothing about. Therefore he has no basis for comparison. There are multitudes of people he does not even know. And even those whom he does know suffer hidden torment which is not revealed to him. Many sorrows lie hidden in the hearts of those who present smiling faces. And many a man has been an object of envy to those who look only upon the surface, and yet to those who know him well, he is more worthy of compassion than envy. If we will consider how little we know of the suffering of others, that realization should silence our own complaints. The early Greek statesman Solon is said to have had a friend who was oppressed with grief, and carried him to a high point overlooking the city of Athens. He showed his friend all the buildings of the city, and said to him, "Consider how

many sorrows there are, have been and will be under those roofs and do not torture yourself with those inconveniences which are common to mankind, as if you alone experienced them." And that was good advice. For suffering is as much a part of our condition as is death itself. Yet we do not see men embitter themselves by the knowledge that they will die; because they see it as both universal and inevitable. They are more likely to say as do the Epicureans, "Let us eat and drink for tomorrow we die." 1 Corinthians 15:32. Why then should we not look upon our afflictions in the same way, and take them as the common lot of humanity, being content to take the advantages and the burdens of that condition together?

2. Beyond the consideration of the unknown calamities of others, if we will but look at those which lie open and visible to us, most of us will find sufficient reason not to complain. Who among us, if he considers his own miseries, may not find many suffered by others which equal or exceed his own? He who considers himself condemned or ignored may readily see others who are persecuted or oppressed. He who groans under some sharp pain may easily see others whose pain is far worse. And even he who suffers the most acute pain in his body, may see others who suffer greater harm from agonies of the mind. So, if we will but look about us, we should see so many persons worthy of our pity and our compassion that we should be ashamed to demand such pity for ourselves.

3. Some may point out that this cannot be universally true, for there must be some lowest state of misery. While I admit that, I would point out that this lowest state more probably consists of a class of people than any one person; and that very few of us could ever claim to be in that class. But these types of comparisons make little sense, for probably no man is as miserable as is possible and the most miserable are by far the minority. No matter how passionately

men may exaggerate their calamities, few would actually change positions with those whom they profess to think are more happy. It was a saying of Socrates that if there were an exchange which held all of men's troubles, most would choose to keep their own rather than to venture upon those of another. And he had good reason for this observation, for when we consider how great a proportion of men's sufferings are of their own making, real or imagined, they may fear lest they should exchange feathers for lead, their own empty shadows for the real and pressing burdens of others. They may consider it best to lift up that which is their own than to carry the burdens of another. We often see that it is minor irritations which make people complain of how unfortunate they think that they are, but that they would not risk exchanging these things for the frustrations of another.

4. Even where the exchange appears to be equal, a prudent man would not likely take the risk. It is no small advantage to know what it is we have to contest with; to have experienced the worst of its attacks and thereby have learned how to defend ourselves. But a new evil comes upon us with the force of surprise and finds us open and disarmed. We have, it seems, almost a miraculous power by experience to have learned how to manage our own attacks. All of our senses have become attuned to them, and while their ugly form may at first startle us, by experience, the terror is averted and we have grown familiar with the harsh sounds and frightful scenes. The effect upon our minds is that we have learned to accept and to manage our own calamities. But if a man were to exchange the old for a new set of such struggles, it would be much like inviting a wild lion into his house to replace a tame one. For all he knows, it may immediately tear him to pieces; or at least cause him great pains to render it gentle and familiar. Certainly, no wise man would want to make such a bargain.

5. It appears then that while we tend to exaggerate our own problems and minimize those of others, we dare not, upon reflection, really accept our own estimation. And what more need be said about our discontents? It is a basic principle of life that everyone will have afflictions. "Man that is born of a woman," says Job, "is of few years and full of trouble." Job 14:1. We would have to reverse this God given fundamental law before we could expect to be exempt from trouble. All that any man can aspire to is but to have a common share with others, and this is true for most. It would be hard for any man to prove otherwise, and until he can, his murmurings are surely unjustifiable; especially when he dares not, upon sober reflection, exchange his afflictions with those of most of his neighbors. He is a poor member of any community who will not pay his fair share of taxes. And he is no better who in the common tax God has laid upon our nature is not content to bear his share.

6. And if we seriously consider that in all our sufferings, nothing falls upon us but that which is common to mankind, and which in fact is greatly exceeded by many of those around us, then surely we must hold to some irrational enjoyment of our own impatience. The Apostle thought it a competent consolation for the early Christians to remind them that "there had no temptation befallen them, but what was common to men." 1 Corinthians 10:13. But we betray our extravagant opinions of ourselves if we think that this is not true for us. Indeed, it would not be possible for us to be so unsatisfied as the majority of us appear to be if we did not cling to creative falsehoods when comparing ourselves to others.

7. We are dishonest with ourselves. We do not fairly compare our good with the good of others, or our troubles with theirs. Instead, with an envious curiosity, we amass together all the desirable circumstances of our neighbors and set that up against the totality of our grievances. This is clearly not

a fair or honest comparison. It is as if I were to compare the length of my arm to the length of another man's finger. And we reverse this strange measurement if we compare our morality to that of another. We pretend that his vices are greater but that his troubles are less. Both comparisons offend any objective sense of reason and justice. A man takes a perverse joy in imagining himself less wicked than his neighbor. But what comfort can he find in imagining himself to be more miserable? How much better it would be if we thought our sufferings to be less than they really are, for it is often our own viewpoint that we recognize and not the reality of things.

8.   If only we could learn to use our eyes correctly and to see things in their true shapes, what a change there would be in our estimates of the world. How many of those shining images which men look upon from a distance with admiration would instead be condemned by them, if only they saw them as they really are. Competency is better than abundance. The pomp of princes that we envy is but an illusion when we see the cares and hazards which attend it. If we saw these things as they really are, men would, like Saul, "hide themselves" I Samuel 10:22 from being chosen; for if we understood the weight of it, we would not choose it. Yet so childishly are we misled by the glittering appearance of things that we think happiness must dwell in mansions. We overlook what lies before us in our humble homes, where happiness would reside if she could but find us there. We are too commonly engaged in a rambling pursuit of her where she is seldom to be found, and in the process we miss her at our own doors.

9.   Indeed, there are few things more foolish and which bring greater unhappiness, which are a part of the very nature of man, than his fond admiration of the enjoyment of others and his contempt of his own. And while we are in that state of mind, it will prevent both our present and our future

contentment. For if we could possess all of those things which we envy that are possessed by others, we would soon find that they had become detestable to us. This is not mere speculation, for many people have pursued their desires with great eagerness and through dangerous hazards only to find that when they have obtained what they sought, it has made them sick. And surely most of us have experienced this at some time and to some degree. Yet so fatally stupid are we that we do not learn from our defeats or alter our estimates concerning the happiness of others. Our comparisons are both unfair and mischievous. If we could begin at the correct starting point, we would look with as much compassion on the adversities of others as we do with envy upon their possessions. Every man would find good cause to sit down contentedly with his own burdens and admit that he bears but his proportionate share of the common weight, unless his own demerits have increased his share of them. In that case, he should marvel that his afflictions are so few rather than so many. Every man knows more of his own ills than those of another, and if he really does exceed others in suffering, then he most likely exceeds others in sins also.

10. If we go beyond the consideration of our contemporaries, and look upon the generations of old, we will find even greater cause to acknowledge God's great indulgence to us. Abraham, though he was the friend of God, was not exempted from severe trials. He was made to wander from his own country and to live the life of a vagrant. And he was made to wait so very long for the fulfillment of the promised offspring that when Isaac was born it caused an uproar in his family which resulted in the expulsion of Ishmael from the family, although he was a son also. And imagine what turmoil of heart he experienced when he was told to sacrifice his son Isaac? Although it was a triumph of his faith, yet surely there could not be a greater pressure upon a human being. David, who is called the man after God's own heart, is no less remarkable for his afflictions than he is for his piety.

He was for a long time an exile from his own country, and what was for him far worse, barred from the temple by the persecutions of Saul. And even after he gained the throne which he had been promised, he suffered a succession of tragedies. There was the incestuous rape of his daughter, the retaliatory murder of Amnon, the conspiracy of Absalom against him, the base revilings of Shimei, and finally the loss of his infant son because of his own sin. He suffered a cluster of afflictions to which ours are, as the prophet said, like the gleanings after the harvest is done. And so it was for many of our forefathers. The Apostle gives us a brief summary, saying, "they had trial of cruel mockings and scourgings; yea moreover, of bonds and imprisonments; they were stoned, were sawn asunder, were tempted, were slain with the sword; they wandered about in sheep skins, and goat skins, being destitute, afflicted, tormented; they wandered in deserts, and in mountains, and in dens, and caves of the earth." Hebrews 11:36-38. And the early Christians suffered in much the same way. They were not spared from calamities, for their whole lives were scenes of suffering. Paul gives an account of his own, "in labor more abundant, in stripes above measure, in prisons more frequent, in deaths often, once I was stoned, thrice I suffered shipwreck, a night and a day have I been in the deep, journeying often," etc. 2 Corinthians 11:23. And if these were his hardships, what would be the sum of those of his fellow laborers? What a noble army of martyrs sealed their faith with their blood and of whose sufferings church history gives us such an astonishing account!

11.   And now "being compassed about with a great cloud of witnesses" says the Apostle in an indisputable argument, "let us run with patience the race which is set before us." Hebrews 11:2. And the argument is even stronger with the further consideration he calls us to, "looking unto Jesus the author and finisher of our faith, who for the joy that was set before Him, endured the cross, despising its shame." Verse

3. Indeed, if we consider His whole earthly life, we see that He was accurately called by the prophet "a man of sorrows." Isaiah 51. And as He took upon Himself all our grief as well as all our sins, there is no human calamity which we may not find exemplified in Him. Does anyone complain of the lowness and poverty of his position? The Lord's whole life was lived in a state of indigence. He lived among animals in the small stable where He was born. And later, He Himself said that He "had nowhere to lay His head." Luke 9:58. Is anyone oppressed by unfair criticism and reproach? Let him consider that his Savior was accused as "a glutton and wine bibber," Luke 7:34, a "blasphemer," John 10:33, a "sorcerer" Matthew 12:24, and a "perverter of the nation." Luke 23:2. In fact, to such a sordid lowness had they reduced His reputation that a seditious thief and murderer was thought to be a more appropriate person to receive mercy; "not this man, but Barabbas." John 18:40. And this awful scene of indignities was clothed with the spiteful pageant of "mockery" acted out by the soldiers, Matthew 27:28, and the barbarous insults of the priests and scribes, verse 41. Is any man despised or deserted by his friends? The Lord was condemned by His countrymen, thought mad by His friends, betrayed by one of His disciples, abandoned by all, and renounced three times by the friend who followed Him the longest. And what is infinitely more than this, He seemed deserted by God also, as shown by His most sorrowful exclamation, "My God, My God, why has thou forsaken me?" Matthew 27:64. Is any man dissatisfied by the hardship and labor of his life? Let him remember that his Savior's was not a life of luxury, where men are "gorgeously appareled and live delicately." Luke 7:25. But He was brought up under the humble roof of a carpenter and subjected to the lowness of that position. He began His prophetic office with the severity of a 40 day fast. And in discharging His ministry, we see that He was in perpetual labor, "going about doing good." Acts 10:38. And this was not in triumph like a prince dispensing

His blessing, but in weary service, riding only once, and that upon a borrowed beast, to fulfil a prophecy. Matthew 24. Does any man groan under sharp and acute pains? Let him consider what his Redeemer endured, and how he "trod the wine press alone." Isaiah 63:3; how He suffered every state of His passion. His arms were bound with rough cords. His head was struck with a stick, and torn with a crown of thorns. His back was plowed with those "long furrows," Psalm 120:3, which the scourges made. His feeble body was oppressed by the weight of His cross, and at last stretched out upon it. His hands and feet, those most sensitive parts, were pierced by nails and His whole body fastened to that accursed tree and exposed naked in a cold season. His throat was parched with thirst and yet afflicted more with vinegar and gall by which they mockingly pretended to relieve Him. And finally He died from these awful torments. Lastly, does any man labor under the most bitter of sorrows, a wounded spirit because of sin? Even in this, he may find that he has an "high priest who hath been touched with the sense of his infirmities." Hebrews 4:15. He was violently assaulted with a succession of temptations, Matthew 4, and we cannot doubt that on Him Satan would employ the utmost of his skill. Nor was He less oppressed with the burden of sin, for He bore ours, not His own. Consider His extreme apprehension in the garden when He so earnestly anticipated that which was His primary purpose in coming into this world. This dreadful pressure wrung from Him bloody sweat, and put Him in inexplicable agony, the horror of which is beyond our comprehension. And finally how awesome was the divine wrath which brought forth from Him His last cry on the cross, Hebrews 5:7, which cry must certainly overwhelm our loudest groans? Let us say with Pilate, "behold the man," or rather with a more holy author, "behold, if ever there were sorrows like unto His sorrows." Lamentations 1:12.

12.   And about these things, Christ Himself said, "if these things be done in a green tree, what shall be done in the dry?" Luke

23:31. If our guilt transferred to Him could draw such severe wrath, what would we expect for ourselves? If we were to judge by human standards, we would expect to receive twice the punishment which He received. Yet such is the effectiveness of His atonement for us that we have been left only a small representative share, that we may demonstrate in our lives our relationship to our crucified Lord. Our sufferings are mere tokens which we wear. If the most afflicted of us were to weigh our sorrows against His, how absurdly unequal would the comparison appear? Therefore, as the best means of battling against our own mutiny, to shame us out of our complaints, let us often consider this unequal comparison, and confront our petty uneasiness with His unspeakable torments, and we will surely find that our admiration and gratitude must replace our impatience.

13. This is indeed the method to which the apostle directs us; "consider Him that endured such contradiction of sinners against Himself, lest ye be weary and faint in your minds: ye have not yet resisted unto blood." Hebrews 12:34. Was He assaulted in so many ways, and yet we expect to be humored and given every little thing which we desire? Did He resist unto death, and yet we think it intolerable to suffer some pressure which wrings a few tears from us? This behavior is so lacking in courage as to render us unfit to follow the Captain of our salvation. What kind of soldier is he who will not share the hazards and hardships of his General? Honest Uriah would not take the comforts of his own house when his commander Joab, who was merely a fellow subject of the king, "lay encamped in the open fields." 2 Samuel 11:11. Shall we forsake our fellow soldiers in pursuit of our own ease and comfort? He has an unworthy attitude who will not follow the example of his superiors. The Roman historian Plutarch tells us that the general Cato, while marching his army through the desert, was in great distress because of thirst. His soldiers brought to him a small quantity of water in a helmet as a great prize, but he refused it, despite the

great generosity of it, because his soldiers could not share it. And when they saw what their commander voluntarily endured for their sakes, their thirst became more bearable for them, and they were ashamed to complain about it. And surely we discredit our Lord if we cannot bear but a small portion of what He endured before us and for us.

14. And let us not make excuses for ourselves because of the weakness of the flesh, saying that we do not have the powers of endurance which the Lord had. Remember the examples of the saints, who were mere men like ourselves, who not only patiently, but willfully, endured many tribulations. By their example, we see that it is not impossible for us also with the common aids of grace to do as they did. For the difference between them and us is not so much in the degree of the aids of grace received, as in the diligence of employing them. Let us therefore, as the apostle advises, "lift up the hands which hang down, and the feeble knees," Hebrews 12:12, and follow the heroic examples which they set before us. And since we see that even these most favored believers suffered severely, let us never think ourselves immune and hold to some flattering hope that we will be spared. Instead, let us remind ourselves in those terms which the Jews used towards our Savior, "art thou greater than Abraham, and the prophets, who makes thou thyself?" John 8:52. And let us also consider the present suffering of our contemporaries, and ask the apostle's question, "what then, are we better than they?" Romans 3:9. If we think that we are, then we may know that we are worse because of the sheer insolence of the thought. And if we admit that we are not, then for what reason should we expect to be better treated? To conclude then, let us not look only upon the evils which we ourselves must bear, but let us look attentively about us and consider what others endure. Let every man cheerfully take his turn in bearing the common burden of mortality until we put off both it and all its appendages together, until this mortal flesh shall put on immortality. 1 Corinthians 15:54.

SECTION X

Of particular aids for the gaining of Contentment

1. We have now passed through all of those considerations which we at first proposed, and must trust the reader to have filled up the subject with his own recollections and considerations. Yet because of the common vice of impatience, those who have the greatest need to meditate upon these matters may be the least willing to do so. Therefore, it may be beneficial to reduce the forgoing into some short directions and rules for the gaining of contentment.

2. The first and most fundamental principle is the mortification of our pride, for it is the garden out of which most sins grow, including the sin of complaint. Men who have a high opinion of themselves cannot be satisfied, for however well they are treated, they still think it short of their merits. Princes often find this to be true of those who have offered them services. But God finds it in those who have offered Him none. We expect that He shall dispense to us according to our own false estimates of ourselves. Therefore, he that aspires to contentment must first take a truer measure of himself. He must consider that he was nothing until God gave Him life, so that He could draw out from that life that which He rightfully expects. And for this reason, there is no

right to receive earthly rewards. Whatever man may receive is an undeserved bounty, and to complain that he does not have more is like the murmurings of an unthankful debtor, who seeks only to increase his debt when he has no ability or intention to ever repay.

3. Secondly, let everyone of us seriously consider how many blessings he enjoys every day, and remember that he has no right to any of them. And let him not miss the clear and obvious fact that these blessings are far greater than those inferior things which he so impatiently seeks after. Let him ask himself if he would really sacrifice what he has to get what he does not have. I suppose that no man in his right mind would do so, his very mind being one of the things he would lose. Let him then consider how unreasonable and irrational his complaints are. And let him confess that he already has the better parts of what is required for worldly happiness, and that no man ever had it all.

4. Thirdly, let us practice the discipline of thanksgiving for all good things which we have received; and that will cure us of our impatience, for it is not possible to be thankful and to complain at the same time. It is most helpful to the development of this discipline to keep a list of all the bounties, protections and deliverances which we have received from God's hand. Every night we should consider both the individual mercies and the sum of them which we have received that day. Anyone who learns to do this will find so many reasons to be thankful that all his discontent will be stifled by the sheer volume of them. And since the acknowledgement of God's mercies is all He seeks in exchange for them, we must consider thankfulness to be an essential duty. He that finds the flow of God's mercies to him to be interrupted should ask himself whether he has failed in this duty, and by his very lack of thankfulness has "turned away good things from him." Isaiah 59:8. And if he finds this to be the case, as all of us no doubt must confess, then he surely cannot

complain, but must wisely reinforce his gratitude for what remains, as the best course of action to regain what he has lost.

5. And his complaints will all the more be silenced if, in the fourth place, he compares the good which he enjoys to the evil which he has done. This is an infallible cure for impatience. For the most holy man living must admit to such sin in himself that by any reasonable measure of judgment would cause him to forfeit any right to all blessings which he has received. As I previously advised keeping a list of blessings received, so I also advise keeping a list of sins committed. There is no doubt that if anyone compares two such lists, he will be astonished to find that both are so long and so full. And he must wonder at God's mercy in continuing his blessings despite all his provocations, and at his own baseness in continuing those provocations despite all the blessings. Indeed, it is simply our own ignorance and blindness to our own sin and failures that makes it even possible that we should complain, even under the most severe trials which God may send upon us. If we would only look honestly upon our own hearts, we would find many great abominations there. And if we merely considered our outward actions which the world may witness, even these would more than balance any heavy pressures which we must bear. When we find ourselves fretting and struggling under our burdens, let us ask ourselves in the words of the prophet, "why doth a living man complain, a man for the punishment of his sins?" Lamentations 3:9. Let us not spend our breath in murmurings and outcries which will only provoke more stripes. Instead, "let us search and try our ways and turn again to the Lord," v. 40, diligently seeking out "that accursed thing" which has caused our stress, and by removing it, find the pathway which leads to mercy. Sadly, this is not what we tend to do. Instead, we accuse everything and everybody and blame the secondary causes of our calamities, or blame God Himself. All the while, as Job

says, "the root of the matter is found in us." Job 19:28. But we shelter and protect ourselves, when the true path out of our miseries lies in sharpening our appreciation of our own sins. The younger son came to think that the lowest position in his father's family was preferable to the place where he found himself. "Make me one of thy hired servants." Luke 15:19. If we had his penitence, we would find his submission also, and calmly attend to the positions in which God has placed us.

6. As every man in his afflictions should search his own heart, so also should he consider by whose hand all events are ordered. "Is there any evil" (meaning punishment) "in the city and the Lord hath not done it?" Amos 3:6. Who are we that we should argue with Him? Shall a man fight against the one who made him? Let the "potsherd strive with the potsherds of the earth." Isaiah 45:9. Man can neither control the power of God nor question His judgment. "Shall not the judge of all the earth do right?" Genesis 18:25. Since we cannot resist Him nor appeal to anyone above Him, the only rational thing we can do is to submit to Him. Not only are we compelled to submit to Him by necessity, but also by our own best interests. For God's dispensations to us are not for the bare purpose of asserting His dominion, but to show His fatherly care for us. He knows our needs and gives to us in accordance with those needs. Because of His essential goodness, He cannot take delight in our distress. "He doth not afflict willingly, nor grieve the children of men." Lamentations 3:33. Therefore, whenever He gives to us a bitter cup, we may know with certainty that the contents are the very medicine which our true infirmities require. He does not trust our appetites and tastes to determine what we need. As the apostle John said, "honey in the mouth may prove gall in the bowels," Revelation 10:9, and cause fatal disease. Let us therefore in our calamities "not consult with flesh and blood," Galatians 1:16, for the more it suffers the more it complains, but look instead to the hand that strikes.

Let us assure ourselves that the stripes we receive are not more than are necessary for our good. And since they are so, then if we are reasonable, they should be our choice as well as His. Not only our faith, but also our self-interest, should promote us to say with old Ely, "it is the Lord, let Him do what seemeth Him good." 1 Samuel 3:18. Unfortunately, we do not understand what is in our own best interests because we do not rightly understand what we are ourselves. We tend to think merely of the animal parts of ourselves and do not realize that when the body suffers it may release the spiritual parts within us, which are besieged and oppressed by the flesh. At best, the body is to the soul like a garment is to the body. And what man would not rather have his clothing cut than his flesh? We may well question our own sanity if we complain that our souls are secured at the cost of our bodies. And this is the most severe design which God has upon us. Our impatient resistance serves only to frustrate His intentions and will not prevent a more severe medicine from being required. Our murmurings may ruin our souls, but they will not prevent our outward calamities.

7.   A seventh help to contentment is to have a right estimate of the world, and of our common human condition. We should consider the world to be merely a stage, and ourselves only as actors upon it. It does not much matter what part we play, but it matters a great deal how well we play it. An actor may draw as much applause from playing one part as another, and may reverse his role the next day. So great is the uncertainty of the world that it makes little sense to build one's hopes upon it. The only thing which is certain about the world is that every condition in it comes with worry and strife, so that when we seek to change our position in it, we are merely seeking to vary rather than to end our miseries. And certainly, anyone who rightly sees the vanity and frustration of the world cannot be much surprised by anything which happens to him in it. We expect no more of any creature but to be what it was created to be. We may as well

be angry that we cannot tame a lion or direct the wind as that we cannot protect ourselves from dangers and disappointments in this rough and mutable world. We may state it as an irrefutable principle that in this vale of tears every man must meet with sorrows and disasters. And we may take our peculiarities and unevenness of temper as merely the natural consequences of being human. And when we think ourselves to suffer more than others, because of the false comparisons which we make, that itself is merely part of our condition. By nature, we use the magnifying glass of discontent and envy to look at our own sorrows and the apparent happiness of others. But we use an opposite glass of ingratitude and lack of compassion to minimize our own blessings and the sufferings of others. And whenever we do this, we cause our own dissatisfactions. He that seeks to make comparisons must do so honestly and sincerely and must view his neighbor's calamities as clearly as he does his own. He must view his own comforts as clearly as those of his neighbor. If we could only do this, we would find that most seeming inequalities are simply not real.

8.   In the eighth place, even when there is no equality, we should remember what a poor thing it is for any man to think himself miserable just because another man appears to be happy. Yet this very thing by itself has made many feel wretched. We tend to create our own desires based solely upon the envious contemplation of the riches possessed by others. How false and evil a thing this is! Even Lucifer was happy enough until he considered that he was "not like the Most High." Isaiah 14:14. And when by his very proud and insolent ambition he had forfeited all personal happiness, and found instead only aggravation and torment, he has ever since sought with all his industry to bring this upon all mankind and to defeat God's purposes in us. And how much has he succeeded in doing so when we cannot be satisfied with any inferior degree of prosperity, and increase our impatience whenever others find enjoyment which we

cannot also attain? And do we then allow the evil one to succeed in us by driving us to actually seek to undermine the happiness of others? Since Satan seeks diligently to impress his own image upon us, we ought to be greatly concerned to guard ourselves by doing just the opposite, and with Christian sympathy for our fellow believers, "rejoice with them that do rejoice." Romans 12:15. By doing so, the comforts of others lift us up as well and do not cause us misery. Love has a strange magnetic power and draws the concerns of our brothers to us, so that he who has love in his heart cannot want for refreshment while any around him are happy. For by adopting their interests, he also shares in their joys. Jethro, although he was an alien, "rejoiced for all the good God had done to Israel." Exodus 18:9. Why should we not have such a sensible unity with our fellow Christians? He that finds such unity will always find a counter balance to his own sufferings.

9.   Let anyone who seeks contentment set boundaries to his desires. It is our common sin that we "enlarge our desires as hell, and cannot be satisfied," Habakkuk 2:5, and then think that God has not treated us well, if He does not fill our insatiable appetites. If we would confine our expectations to those things which we actually need, or which God has promised to us, few of us indeed would not find them abundantly answered. Consider that there are few things which we actually need, although there may be many that we want. And it is relatively rare to lack actual necessities. In fact, most of us have much in addition to our necessities which God has given to us for our delight and our pleasure. Yet God's promises which we find in the Gospel extend only to those necessities. Christ assured His disciples that "these things shall be added unto you." Matthew 6:33. The context apparently shows that He had in mind by the term "these things" only meat and drink and clothing. Therefore, He said, take "no thought for the life what you shall eat, or what you shall drink, nor yet for the body what you shall

put on," verse 25. On what basis may we claim any right to more than this? God never promised honor to the ambitious or luxuries to the covetous or pleasure to the lustful. Let us therefore, if we seek satisfaction, learn in all modesty to confine our desires to the limits which He has set for us. Then every additional gift which He gives to us will appear to be what it really is, a luxury and a bounty. For if we keep expanding our appetites with every gift we receive, then we shall never be satisfied. And if we complain before God and continually ask for more, then we are doing what poets have described as an element of hell, trying to fill a sieve with water or to roll a large stone up a steep mountain.

10.   It is greatly helpful in finding contentment to confine our thoughts to the present, and not let them run ahead to future events. If we could just do this, we could shake off much of our burden. For we often add great weights upon ourselves by anxiety over things which may never happen. And we sink more under those loads than we do under anything real. This is surely very foolish, for either the hard thing will come or it will not. And if it does, it is not so desirable a guest that we should go out to meet it. We shall encounter it soon enough when it arrives. We need not project by anticipation our sense of it. And if it does not come, then what madness it is for a man to torment himself with that which will never be, and to make himself as miserable as he could be if it were upon him. Often this is all we get by our so called foresight. Seeing the future is one of God's attributes, not ours. We find that our forecasts of the future are usually wrong, and this is as true of our fears as it is of our good expectations. Since we are by nature blind and short sighted, let us not make ourselves out to be scouts, seeking to discover danger at a distance. The odds are that we will only bring home false alarms. Instead, let us find rest in the words of our Lord, "sufficient unto the day is the evil thereof." Matthew 6:34. Let us apply ourselves to the present with all Christian courage, and trust the future to God's hands. When we must look

forward, let it be in obedience to our duty and set our minds on those things which we know to be real, death, judgment, heaven and hell. For the more that we consider these things, the less sensitive we become to mere transitory matters and the less we fear earthly struggles. For it is our neglect of the eternal that exposes us to the fear of the temporary.

11. Lastly, let us overcome all our anxieties and fears by that most effectual remedy which the apostle prescribes; "is any man afflicted? Let him pray." James 5:13. This surely is the most rational thing to do, for what else can we do about our sorrows? We, who have so little power over anything, cannot make "one hair white or black." Matthew 5:36. What can we really do about our condition, or the world around us? Our fears only increase the weight of our burdens. But prayer can give us relief. "Call upon me," says God, "in time of trouble, and I will hear thee and thou shalt praise me." Psalm 50:15. Whenever we are sinking in the floods of affliction, let us support ourselves by presenting our needs to the God of grace and cry out to Him. This is what the apostle Peter did, Matthew 14:30, for God will "take us by the hand, and be the winds" never so "boisterous or contrary," He will protect us from sinking. The winds of this troublesome world will serve but to toss us closer into His arms, who can with a word calm the greatest storm and rescue us from it. Let us not then do actual harm to ourselves by neglecting this infallible means of deliverance! Let us with the psalmist take our refuge under the "shadow of the divine wings, till the calamity be over past." Psalm 57:1. And as this is a sure remedy in our greatest afflictions, it is also a good test of who we really are. Are we upset over mere trifles? Do we argue and complain when our worldly and fleshly desires are not met? Are we discontented when we do not receive what we wish for? No man who seriously considers who it is he prays to would dare insert these requests into his prayers. It is an insult to God to call upon Him for that which is meaningless or evil. We should seriously consider the requests which

we place before Him. When we have done that, we will find that we have already made a judgment about our desires, as to whether they are frivolous or wicked. And if we find them to be so, then we cannot continue to cling to them, but must dismiss them instead. God cares about our real miseries, but not about our imagined ones. Let us not create for ourselves some non-existent disease which we would be ashamed to describe to a doctor. For those diseases which are real, the Apostle Paul's prescription is a universal remedy: "Be careful for nothing, but in everything by prayer and supplications, with thanksgiving, let your requests be made known to God." Philippians 4:6.

SECTION XI

Of Resignation

1. If one truly considers and applies the foregoing principles, he will find them sufficient to enable him to face almost any calamity. But it is human nature to frustrate all sufficient remedies by simply not using them. We are quite willing to talk about our problems, but not willing to do what is necessary to resolve them. I urgently ask the reader to consider that mere knowledge does not by itself affect the issues. That knowledge must be applied by action, or it becomes merely a form of entertainment. And more than this, to know what is needed and to fail to act upon it merely adds to our guilt and thus to our misery.

2. It is well known that many take up books in the same way that they take up a deck of cards or a pair of dice; merely as a diversion or an escape from reality. If a book is read merely to entertain one's sense of curiosity, to see what may be said upon a subject, then it matters little whether the material in it is sound or ridiculous. It is one thing to read a novel that way, but quite another to read in this manner a book about serious spiritual issues. How many good spiritual works have had little effect upon their readers who simply read them for knowledge or entertainment, but never applied them to their lives. Whoever considers a serious practical

subject, ought to do so with the intent to conform his life to what he believes to be his duty. For if he does not, then he will benefit very little from all his reading.

3.   One would think that this warning would not be necessary, as it is the intent of this writing to help people to find contentment. And anyone who reads it might be assumed to be as earnest about the subject as the writer could be. After all, it is in everyone's interest to find the greatest degree of happiness which may be found in this world. Yet I doubt that many will take this pursuit as seriously as they do other spiritual concerns.

4.   Yet it is true that a dissatisfied and complaining attitude is one of the most stubborn and ugly habits of mankind. And as the worst people are often the ones who are most in love with themselves, so also is this ugly habit the most likely to excuse and justify itself. Melancholy is the most stubborn and unmovable of all moods. Discontent is an offspring of that and just as inflexible. It is often unassailable by both reason and faith. In a sullen mood, Jonah justified his discontent even to God Himself, who calmly reproved him, "dost thou well to be angry?" Jonah 4:9. Jonah chose "to be angry even to the death." Do we not see men who are so disappointed and impatient that they grow angry even at their blessings which should comfort them? Their friends, their family and their possessions become so distasteful to them that in their frantic discontent, they will throw away that which is most valuable to them. And this attitude is nearly impossible to defeat. It nourishes itself upon illusions and pretense. And while this is clear to others, it is not visible to the one caught up in it, because he does not want to see the truth, and will only seek out those opinions which agree with him. In addition to this, men will also cherish their sense of suffering and devote all of their thoughts to their grief. There could not be a more absurd contradiction in the world than to hear men cry out because of their burdens

and yet cling to those burdens as if their very lives depended upon it. The first thing which is necessary for men to be cured of their discontent is for them to want to be.

5.   This may look like a paradox, and a man may say that he wants nothing more than to find happiness. He that is poor thinks that he will be cured by wealth. He that is obscure thinks that he will be cured by honor. He will find that a drink is not a real cure for an insatiable thirst, but that the thirst itself must be cured. No outward possession will ever fully satisfy our cravings. Our appetites must be tamed and reduced or they will forever cause torment. And only he who deals with the appetite itself can be said to have been cured.

6.   He who acknowledges the reality of his desires and learns to seek contentment in its proper place may indeed find it. Throughout history, men and women have accepted the grace of God and the true reason which flows from it and found peace and contentment, even in the face of great pressure and torment. They have preserved a serenity of mind by disregarding all such assaults. And this should be a natural sign of our faith.

7.   I do not here recommend a stoical insensitivity which makes no distinctions between the things which happen to us. Some have falsely seen that to be a virtue. No, what I recommend is a superiority of mind which rises us above our sufferings, but does not prevent us from sensing them. We cannot seek any purpose or pattern other than that which was demonstrated for us by our Lord. He had a full and complete sense of all which He experienced. We see this in His earnest plea, "Father, if it be possible let this cup pass." Yet the turmoil of His flesh was overcome by the resignation of His spirit when He said, "nevertheless not what I will, but what Thou wilt." Luke 22. When we imitate this pattern, and in spite of the reluctance of the flesh, yet willingly submit ourselves to His will, we will experience sadness. Yet we will

not be impatient, for we will not be sad for long. To him that is thus "resigned, light will spring up." Psalm 97:11. Some good angel will be sent to us as was sent to our Savior, or God will send some other friend, or provide such internal comfort and support which will counter balance those afflictions which He does not remove.

8.   Indeed, the great purpose of God in correcting us is the same as a wise parent with a child, to break our wills, which are so stubborn that they do not bend to an easy touch, but require substantial force. The rough handling is not finished until we have become compliant to His will. It is therefore very much in our interests to cooperate with His design, and to try to actually assist in the purpose of subjugating our unruly and stubborn willfulness. Let us be wise and choose to quickly resign ourselves to His will so that He will not find further correction to be necessary.

9.   And truly, this is the way to find both peace with God and peace within ourselves. For it is when our stubborn wills take precedence over our reason that confusion and turmoil arise within us. The only possible way to prevent this is to commit our very wills to His safe custody, who alone can order the unruly wills of sinful men. And indeed, experience shows us fully that serenity of the soul is found in resignation to the will of God. He who has done so need no longer worry about his choices. He has no anxiety over future events. For he knows that nothing can happen apart from the will of God, in which he has placed all of his trust. God will choose for him with all the tender regard of a faithful guardian for his ward, or a loving father for his child who throws himself into His arms. There is certainly no greater method to bring us close to God than for us to fully resign ourselves to Him and to His will. We see that the Gibeonites saved themselves by choosing to become servants to the Israelites. Joshua 10:6. Can we think that God is less considerate of His dependents? Both His honor and His compassion

are fully satisfied by granting relief to those who have surrendered themselves to Him.

10. And more even than this, by resignation we unite our wills to the will of God, and this changes everything. When our wills stood alone, we found only continual defeat. But when our wills are united with God's will, we cannot fail, for then the same omnipotence which backs His will also supports ours. For God's will cannot be controlled or resisted. True security is found in this uniting of wills. Any calamities which we encounter, no matter how repugnant to our sensitive natures, may yet be agreeable to our spirits when they have become our choice, since they are certainly His choice, and we have acknowledged His right to make those choices for us. Any adversity, no matter how difficult, may in this light look pleasing. Every day we observe that men will contently accept adversity and struggle if it comes in pursuit of their own wills. If we have really made God's will our own, then we will embrace the hardship which accompanies it cheerfully. There is far greater peace in submitting to and joining in the will of God than there is hardship to our flesh in doing so.

11. Here then is that solid ground upon which we may stand, and do that of which Archimedes boasted, and move the entire world. The whole course of earthly things become subject to us, for all its calamities cease to interfere with the course we pursue. In a sense, we are doing as the prophet said, we are "beating swords into plough-shares, and spears into pruning hooks." Isaiah 2:4. The most hostile weapons and the most adverse events shall become for us instruments of fertility and only advance our spiritual growth.

12. Can we not agree that this is a far better state to be in than to be always harassed by anxieties and fears about the future or to be distraught about the past? And is it not madness or enchantment for us to act contrary to our own desires as well as to our reason and experience? Should we not rather see

and acknowledge the unexplainable happiness of a resigned will, than to hold onto our own wills for the perverse and melancholy pleasure of opposing God and tormenting ourselves? Let us therefore, if not out of duty or even because it is easier, at least for the sake of our own reputations, be men of sobriety and common sense, and do that which is in truth what is in our own best interests. Let us sacrifice our own wills and with them all our fruitless anxieties. Let us cast our burdens upon Him who invites us to do so. He who bears all our sins will bear also all our sorrows and grief, if we will only be content to give them to Him. He will free us from all those oppressive weights which make "our souls cleave to the dust," Psalm 119:25, and will in exchange for them give us only His "light and pleasant burden." Matthew 11:30. In a word, we shall have no remaining cares except to keep ourselves in His care. Let us make our love for Him secure and we are promised that "all things shall work together for our good." Romans 8:28. To conclude, resignation and contentment are virtues, and they are linked together as the cause and the effect. Let us be certain of our resignation and contentment will flow into us without further effort. On the contrary, whenever our wills are in defiance to God's will, we shall always find circumstances and events to be contrary to and in frustration of our wills. Nothing we do can mold them to fit our desires. Instead, we must mold ourselves until we can compliantly and pleasantly say, "it is the Lord, let Him do what seemeth Him good." 1 Samuel 3:18.

SECTION XII

The Close

1. This short rendition of *The Art of Contentment* cannot draw to a more natural and desirable conclusion than with our placing ourselves in the very heart of the divine providence. As the final sign of triumph, Roman conquerors went to their capitol and laid their garlands in the lap of Jupiter. In a similar way, a Christian must put his crown of thorns, which is the trophy of his victory, into the arms of his gracious God. It is there that he places all of his fears, his wants, his sorrows and his very self, which is the best possible repository.

2. The gospel instruction of "not caring for the morrow," Matthew 6:34, and being "careful for nothing," Philippians 4:6, might at first appear to be an abandonment to all of the calamities of life. But consider that we are directed to "cast all our care" upon a gracious and all-powerful Father and are assured that "He cares for us," 1 Peter 5:7. And "tho' a woman may forget her sucking child, that she should not have compassion of the son of her womb, yet will He not forget" His children. Isaiah 49:15. This alone will overcome any objection. While the men of this world trust in human strength, lay up "treasures on earth," a prey for "rust and moth," Matthew 6:19, and a "torment" to themselves, James 5:3, the Christian has omnipotence for his support. He has

"a treasure in Heaven, where no thief approaches, nor moth corrupts," Matthew 6:20. While some theologians will try to fit God's secret will into their theological systems and expect Him to act as they predict, yet the pious man in awe and surrender will submit to what God reveals when He reveals it. He resolves always to obey and never to dispute. For the beloved disciple simply laid his head upon the Lord's breast, while the thief and traitor sought only what he thought he could take from Him.

3.	It is surely a modest demand that the Lord makes upon us. He requires only that we should give Him as much authority as every peasant claims in his own cottage, to be master there, and to dispose of his household as he thinks best; to "say to this man, go, and he goeth; to another, come, and he cometh; and to His servant, do this, and he doth it." Matthew 8:9. If we would but give to Him this liberty, it would put an end to all clamor and complaint.

4.	We must make it our daily prayer that "the will" of God "may be done on earth as it is in Heaven," in a steady, swift, uninterrupted and constant manner. It is a very great rebellion to set up our wills against His. And it is an insane perversity to pray that His will be done, to see it done in contrast to our own wills, and then to complain. We must be very conscious to follow God and not the direction of the heathens all around us. We must not prejudge what God is doing when it does not appear to be what we intended or expected. Instead, in all modesty, let us conform our thoughts to His, and "hearken what the Lord God will say concerning us, for He will speak peace unto His people, and to His saints that they turn not again." Psalm 85:8.

5.	And should any of us fall into sin and indulge some passionate affection, and find ourselves doting upon the illegitimate child, our most precious sins and follies, as David did upon that child who was the result of murder and adultery, yet when the child is taken away, let us do as David did, and rise from our sullen posture and "worship in the house of the Lord." 2 Samuel 12:20. It would be good for us to "lay our hand upon our mouth, because it was His doing." Psalm 39:10. And let us say, as did Job when charged with his murmurings, "behold I am vile, what shall I answer: Once I have spoken, but I will not answer: yea twice, but I will proceed no farther." Job 40:4-5.

6.   Socrates rightly said about contentment that it is in opposition to the seeking of fame and fortune; but that it is the very wealth of nature for it gives to us both what we really want and what we actually need. As believers, we know that resignation to God is the richest of graces because from it flows not only all things that the Christian needs, but also all things that he desires, especially God Himself. For He is indeed the very objective happiness itself of all things which He has created. He who is the source of all being is also the source of all blessedness. And while it is true that we can only receive His blessings in their fullness when we have put off that "flesh which cannot enter into the Kingdom of God," and laid aside that "corruption" which cannot "inherit incorruption," 1 Corinthians 15, yet even in this life, we may come ever closer to that blessed state by acts of resignation and by denial of ourselves. When Socrates was about to die, he said to his friends, "O Crito, since it is the will of God, so let it be. Anytus and Melitus may kill me, but they cannot hurt me." Such resignation as this is a far greater duty for a Christian, and it is also a firm and secure place. Remember that not only martyrs, but Jesus Himself was persecuted. And it was He who said that anyone who opposed Him would find "it hard to kick against the pricks." Acts 9:5.

7.   There could perhaps be no greater example of shameless sensuality than that of the Israelites who murmured for leeks and onions, Numbers 11:5, when they had the food of angels rain down from Heaven for them. No soul that is truly sensitive to God's favor can complain because of any

earthly pressure. "The Lord is my shepherd," said David, "therefore I lack nothing." Psalm 23:1. And he also said, "Thou has put gladness into my heart, more than when their corn, and wine, and oil increased." Psalm 4:7. In passionate rapture he cried out "whom have I in Heaven but Thee? And there is none upon earth that I desire in comparison of Thee. My flesh and my heart faileth, but God is the strength of my heart, and my portion forever." Psalm 46:1 and following. "God is our hope and strength, a very present help in trouble. Therefore will we not fear, tho' the earth be moved, and tho' the hills be carried into the midst of the sea. Tho' the waters thereof rage and swell, and tho' the mountains shake at the tempest of the same. If God be in the midst of us, we shall not be removed, He will help us, and that right early." Let us therefore rest in His support, and as the prophet advises, Isaiah 8:12, "neither fear, nor be afraid," in any urgent and pressing situation no matter how great, "but be still and quiet, and sanctify the Lord of Hosts Himself, and let Him be our fear, and let Him be our dread."

THE END